SUPERNATURAL™

THE OFFICIAL COMPANION
SEASON 1

SUPERNATURAL:
THE OFFICIAL COMPANION SEASON 1
ISBN-10: 1 84576 535 4
ISBN-13: 9781845765354

Published by
Titan Books
A division of
Titan Publishing Group Ltd
144 Southwark St
London, SE1 0UP

First edition August 2007
2 4 6 8 10 9 7 5 3 1

Supernatural ™ & © 2007 Warner Bros. Entertainment Inc.

Visit our website:
www.titanbooks.com

DEDICATION
Dedicated to Thya, whose belief in me has been supernatural.

ACKNOWLEDGEMENTS
Thanks are owed to many people for their contributions to this book. First and foremost, to Eric
Kripke and everyone who graciously gave up their limited time to be interviewed, without whom
this book would not be possible; Amanda Bartley, Diana Kania, Holly Ollis, Winson Seto, and Ben
Tucker for their tireless coordination; Ivan Hayden (and Stargate Digital), Randy Shymkiw, and
Jerry Wanek for the visual materials; Adrien van Viersen for the artwork; my family for their
unwavering support; and to my editors, Jo Boylett at Titan Books and Chris Cerasi at DC Comics,
who made the process extremely smooth and enjoyable.

Titan Books would like to thank the cast and crew of *Supernatural*, Eric Kripke for the Foreword,
Adrien van Viersen for the conceptual art and storyboards on pages 7, 9, and color section 4 and 5,
and Chris Cerasi at DC Comics.

Did you enjoy this book? We love to hear from our readers. Please email us at:
readerfeedback@titanemail.com or write to Reader Feedback at the above address.

To subscribe to our regular newsletter for up-to-the-minute news, great offers and competitions,
email: **titan-news@titanemail.com**

A CIP catalogue record for this title is available from the British Library.

Printed and bound in the United States of America.

SUPERNATURAL™

THE OFFICIAL COMPANION
SEASON 1

Supernatural created by Eric Kripke

NICHOLAS KNIGHT

TITAN BOOKS

CONTENTS

FOREWORD

Here's a question — really, one of the big ones. God knows we ask it enough on *Supernatural*. So, where do you come out: are we living in a chaotic universe, or an ordered one? Are we all just bumping into each other randomly... or does everything happen for a reason?

Here's the thing: I was a comedy writer. It took me several years to realize... I wasn't a particularly good one. None of my scripts came close to production. I was trapped in what they call Development Hell. But it's much more like purgatory.

I got so frustrated that I wrote a horror movie. I was a rabid fan of the genre. I consider the three best movies ever made to be *Citizen Kane*, *Casablanca*, and *Evil Dead II*. But I had never written a horror flick before. However, I needed to blow off some steam and murder some people in the goriest ways possible, and a horror script seemed the most sensible and legal way to do it. I named every victim after a studio executive. I had no further designs on the script; it was solely a therapeutic exercise. But a friend showed it to a friend, and within a year, it was my first produced screenplay. Now, it's by no means a great movie, probably not even a good one. But still, it got made, and after years of struggling, that meant something to me.

And suddenly, I was a horror writer.

Soon after, I had the opportunity to pitch Warner Bros. on a pilot. Now, I had an idea that I'd been mulling over since college, hell, since fifth grade: a series about urban legends. We have a folklore as rich as any world mythology, as American as jazz or baseball, and few people know it. Gory, twisty stories that illuminate our culture, our character. They've long been an obsession of mine... and I've always dreamed of somehow turning them into a movie or TV show. I tried to pitch the idea many times before, but it continually fell on deaf — or at least uninterested — ears. Perhaps the market wasn't right. Or perhaps no one wanted to buy a gory, twisty series from a guy who wrote sub-par Adam Sandler rip-offs.

But suddenly, I was a horror writer.

And suddenly, the market was right for horror. And so I pitched Warner Bros. on my idea, an idea I'd slaved over, the kind of fragile idea you cup in your hands so it won't be crushed.

It was about a reporter who investigated urban legends.

Warner Bros. hated it.

They asked if I had anything else. I didn't. Nothing. All I had were a few words I'd scrawled in my notebook on a whim, literally the day before. I'm looking at it right now. Here it is: "One way you could do this show would be two guys on a road trip, cruising the country. 'Route 66' style. Brothers?" I had nothing else to say to Warner Bros., so I said this.

Ever since, I've been working full time — damn near twenty-four/seven — on *Supernatural*. It's at times painful and frustrating... I've barely seen my impossibly patient and beautiful wife over the past three years... but god help me, I love my job. I'm passionate about the subject matter. I believe in the characters. I'm proud of Jared and Jensen — they can handle anything we throw at them; on top of that, they're truly good, smart, down to earth guys. I have the pleasure of working with Bob Singer, Kim Manners, Phil Sgriccia, Cyrus Yavneh, John Shiban, Sera Gamble, Raelle Tucker, Jerry Wanek, Serge Ladouceur, and many, many others who have deepened and expanded and improved this show beyond my wildest expectations.

Supernatural is a modest, little, under-the-radar series... but it's still a dream come true for me. And for the first time in my career, I'm having the time of my life. And I get to do things I never thought I'd do in a million years — like write Forewords for episode guides, as an example.

Now, I don't know if the universe is an ordered one, if everything happens for a reason... and anyone who claims to know for sure is lying. But when I look back at the winding, precarious path that led me to *Supernatural*, well... it sure as hell seems like it.

Eric Kripke
April 2007

Below
Adrien van Viersen's conceptual painting of the Woman in White, for 'The Pilot'.

MANIFESTING SUPERNATURAL

DEAN: I think he wants us to pick up where he left off. You know, saving people, hunting things... the family business.

"In the beginning, the story was just a delivery system to get into the urban legends," *Supernatural* creator Eric Kripke reveals. "Then the show evolved way beyond that as we got into the characters."

As he explains in the Foreword, Kripke has always loved urban legends and American folklore, and has wanted to bring them to the screen in some form for over ten years. "The very first idea was to do it as a feature film and combine all these urban legends into one film," Kripke recalls. He is, of course, aware that there's already been a movie called *Urban Legends* (1998). He found the movie frustrating, not because they'd beaten him to the punch, but because "they didn't do supernatural or do the real urban legends. To just use urban legends as the m.o. for a serial killer drove me nuts.

"Then I wanted to do an anthology series. Then I wanted to do it with a bunch of tabloid writers in a van driving around the country," Kripke continues. "It was a good thing that the reporter idea that I'd spent months and months on was shot down," he concludes, referring to the fact that *Night Stalker*, a horror series about reporters investigating supernatural activities, debuted on ABC at the same time as *Supernatural* — and failed to survive its first season.

But while Kripke was ecstatic that Warner Bros. wanted to do the Route 66 version of his urban legends series, at first he was "very resistant of the idea because of its production demands. I said, 'Never in a million years are you guys going to make this series because there are no standing sets and it's a different location every time.'" Fortunately, he got the head of production's guarantee, and the series moved forward.

"We put a pitch together and took it to all the networks. The WB made the strongest agreement." Then Kripke got to work on the first script... and it was a figurative car wreck: "I handed it in to the studio just before Thanksgiving. 'We don't like it. We don't want to show it to the network.'" Naturally, that's not at all what Kripke had expected to hear. But upon reflection, he realized that the script — which had Dean trying to convince Sam that monsters are real, after the boys had grown up with an aunt and uncle away from their demon-hunting father — had "a really complicated back-story for people to relate to. It got confusing and had so much exposition. I sat down with Peter Johnson, and we talked about what we could do to salvage this.

"McG and Peter Johnson were involved from the beginning," Kripke explains. "It helps to have someone with McG's muscle behind the project."

When they first formed their partnership, co-executive producer Peter Johnson told Kripke, "Whatever spooky idea you want to do, I'm down with that."

Johnson and Kripke brainstormed well together, and 'The Pilot' was saved. "One

Opposite

A selection of Adrien van Viersen's storyboards for Sam's encounter with the Woman in White in 'The Pilot'.

Above

Sam and Dean
Winchester's
'discussion' gets
interrupted in 'The
Pilot'.

way to short-circuit all that confusing back-story is to have them raised with their father, and that was sort of the light-bulb moment," Kripke recalls. "What if he raised them on the road? He just took them with him... That opened up this whole realm of possibilities. Now they can be amazing fighters and really great at conning people, and there'd be no building they couldn't get into. And you won't have to have these long conversations about 'Hey dude, ghosts are real.' They're basically like blue-collar exterminators. So we went back to the WB and pitched it, and they loved it."

Of course, Kripke still had to write the new pilot script... before Christmas. He cancelled all his holiday plans and locked himself in his office. "I said, 'Screw it. If I'm giving up my holiday plans, I'm going to get loose with it.' And I threw in references like the Mulder and Scully lines. I looked at it and said, 'My god, it's a better script.' The network liked it — I'm not going to say they flipped over it."

In fact, the script didn't get green-lit until preeminent pilot director David Nutter came onboard. "David Nutter was definitely our knight in shining armor," Kripke says. "When he said, 'Okay, I'm in,' I turned to Peter Johnson and said, 'Not only did our pilot just get green-lit, but our series just got picked up!' David signed on at 11am and we were picked up by 2pm."

"The thing that really brought me to the project," says Nutter, "was the relationship, what the characters are all about. This is a story of brothers whose mother dies a horrible death and now they're searching for their father. So in a pilot situation, that's a story I can get involved with — that's the heartbeat of the show."

For 'The Pilot', it was all about casting the parts of Dean and Sam Winchester. "It doesn't matter how good the script is if the lead actors aren't appealing," says Kripke. "The first person we got serious about was Jensen." They wanted to find a "young Harrison Ford" and Kripke believes they found him in Jensen Ackles. "Jensen's as charismatic as he is on screen, and you latch on to him and want to watch him."

They met with Jared Padalecki next. "My wife's a huge fan of *Gilmore Girls* and Jared's just so likeable." Thing was, they'd originally put Jensen on tape as Sam. "We called Jensen's rep and said, 'He might not be Luke Skywalker, but he gets to be Han Solo!' And they were cool with that." In fact, everyone was cool with it.

"It was nice knowing that Jared and I were everybody's first choice," comments Jensen Ackles. "They didn't even bring in anybody else."

The network executives would've been asleep at the wheel to miss the brotherly chemistry and easy friendship the two young Texan actors formed. "Though he and I both play similar roles, I find myself so happy when something's happening for him," says Jared Padalecki about his camaraderie with Ackles, "and I know when something's happening for me, he's also so happy."

Even David Nutter, with his extensive experience in the industry, was blown away by Padalecki and Ackles's chemistry. "Never have I done a show where two actors clicked so well together. These guys had never met each other before and it was like they were brothers."

In discussing the setting of 'The Pilot', Kripke explains, "I chose Lawrence [Kansas] because of its proximity to Stull Cemetery, which is sort of a famous haunted cemetery where there's some really cool urban legends." Indeed, it's often referred to as a "gateway to hell". Like Sam, Kripke describes himself as the "black sheep youngest son" that goes to California and leaves the family business behind. But he didn't leave his roots far behind, as the overall vibe of the show attests. "I'm from a kind of industrial factory town in Ohio called Toledo. I think there's a real Midwest sensibility that I bring to the show that came from my living there, the guys I grew up with — my proximity to blue-collar guys and blue-collar lifestyles. I really love that these are Midwestern heroes driving in a muscle car. They're more comfortable in small towns and greasy diners, and so am I. They kind of live the life that I understand more: beer and cheeseburgers and dive bars."

And the music featured in the show is likely to be playing from tinny speakers in said dive bars. "My friends call me 'Old Man Kripke' because I don't like any band that's recorded after 1980. There's a real energy in the Midwest to miles and miles of flat farmland and two-lane blacktop that stretches into infinity and you're jamming classic rock as loud as it can go. There's something so mythic, so American about that, and that's the energy I wanted the show to have. It was so important that the show have this ass-kicking soundtrack." So important that he said to Warner Bros., "I swear, if you change the music on this show I'm walking off it."

"The music plays such an integral role," comments composer Christopher Lennertz. "It's more like a movie where there's a lot of music and there's a lot of different score and there's scary stuff and emotional stuff." Lennertz, whose score for 'The Pilot' received an Emmy nomination, alternates episodes with composer Jay Gruska, who says, "I don't know a composer who doesn't have fun with 'the evil that

DID YOU KNOW?

In one version of the pilot script that Eric Kripke turned in to the studio, the episode ended with the boys finding their dad dead on the ceiling.

Above

Sam and Dean shine a light on the supernatural things that go bump in the night.

lurks'... That's really fun to do musically."

While the music's become a signature of the show, there's no denying it has a distinct visual signature as well. Kripke attributes a lot of the credit for the show's look to Aaron Schneider, director of photography on 'The Pilot'. "Aaron wasn't afraid of darkness, and that's what I think was the most exciting thing he brought to the table. Every TV exec we've worked with has asked for the show to be lighter. Aaron was not afraid to light a dark show and light them in silhouette, and let them fall away in the shadows. The fact is that scary moments have to be scary and scary plays in the darkness. When the boys first had that fight in Sam's apartment, it's all done silhouetted against the backlit window. That's really daring. I'm proud as hell of the work he did on 'The Pilot'."

The work everyone did on 'The Pilot' was phenomenal, so it's no surprise *Supernatural* got picked up for a series. At that point, according to Kripke, the studio said he needed to partner with an executive producer with production experience. They paired him with Robert Singer, which Kripke describes as being "like an arranged marriage, because you're going to be working more closely with that person than anyone else. It's worked out beyond both of our expectations." Robert Singer concurs. "We're very much of the same mind, Eric and I, and I think that he fills in certain gaps I have and I fill in certain gaps he has." Kripke feels that Singer doesn't get nearly the credit he deserves for the complexity he brings to the show when filling in those gaps. "He is the one who really demands the characters have depth."

The studio also wanted Kripke to bring in someone to help build the mythology, to build stories, to work with the writers, so "David told Eric, 'Get Shiban in here,'" remembers co-executive producer John Shiban. "So we met and immediately clicked." Shiban brought years of *The X-Files* experience to the table, and with regards to mythology, he posed the question, "Can you build a boat that will still float, but without all its pieces? Because… there are discoveries that are going to be made along the way, there'll be characters that you stumble on." The idea of Meg, who turned out to be very central to the mythology as an undercover demon, was a perfect example of that.

They started hiring staff writers as soon as the series was picked up, and Kripke hit the ground running, ready to dive into the lore he so adores. "I showed up the first day of work with eighty urban legends that were my favorites." For the first batch of episodes, the legends tended to come first. "I had a pile that I really wanted to do," Kripke explains. "The storylines of the boys came later. But once we realized how good they were and the depth of storytelling we could tell about them, we really began to focus more on what their issues were, and what interesting story we wanted to tell about them."

With their focus flipped, they started to only use urban legends that fit with the boys' story. And Kripke thinks the second half of season one was better than the first half because of that. "Obviously the brother relationship has become the heart of everything," Kripke continues. "If it was just two guys, there'd be no psychological dimension to go to because guys just punch each other in the shoulder and tell fart jokes. We're a family drama that just happens to have demons and monsters in it, but the demons and monsters only serve to illustrate the internal demons that they're facing."

Of course, there is a drawback to putting a family drama at the heart of an action-horror show. "We always end up having more chick-flick moments than we'd like," Kripke says ruefully. "But they're a little unavoidable once you start living with these characters, and if you're interested in illuminating what's painful and vulnerable about them." Nonetheless, they tend to try to find ways to tell the emotional storylines in a way that's not… "'wussy'. The trick that took us a while to learn is that it's not what they say, it's what they *don't* say. It's about more mature writing and understanding the boys better."

Regardless of which part of season one he speaks about, Kripke is always animated. "I'm just so passionate and proud of it. Because I do love the legends so much and I have an affinity with the characters, and because the show has the freedom to be funny. It's a really, really fun show to write."

GIRLFRIENDS ARE EVIL

The studio wanted Jessica to be in the story more, to be an ongoing character in the series, "but there just wasn't a place for 'Sam, I love you. When are you coming home?'" reveals Eric Kripke. "So I said, 'Let's kill Jessica!' And they said, 'Okay, that's cool. You won't see that coming.'" Then they made her *evil*. "We went on a detour for a while where Sam came home and realized that Jessica was a demon implanted in his life and then she vanished or smoke came out of her and he realized the demons were much closer to him than he ever thought, and that sends him out on the road. I think in the last five pages in the pilot, that's a tough aspect to sell. What felt like the right bookends were mom's death and then Jessica's death, and they died in the same way. It always ends up being what it needs to be."

Above

One of Sam and Dean's many memorable motel rooms.

As he hinted earlier, when he described getting "loose" with the revised pilot script, Kripke concurs that he always wanted humor in *Supernatural*. "A lot of shows are so relentlessly dark that they're not fun to watch. At the end of the day, what's important is that this is a popcorn show and it's fun to watch. To have a smartass like Dean in the middle of all this who can just say anything you want him to say is great."

They make a point of balancing the humor with the family drama with the monster-of-the-week, and Johnson recalls that "about halfway into the season, all those elements gelled together." Yet, Singer is quick to say that they "don't do it formulaically. We kind of let the story take us where it wants to go. Then we can finish it and go, 'I think we can use some more scares,' or 'We can use a big thing at the end of act two,' or something like that. We put the writers through a lot of hoops getting the stories right."

One of those writers, Raelle Tucker, thinks it's more than worth it. "What's special about *Supernatural* is that it has the ability to make you laugh, scream, and then cry, all in the same episode, all within seconds of each other, which is a really specific type of thing. I can't think of another show that does that."

Although 'The Pilot' was shot in Los Angeles, the series moved to Vancouver, British Columbia, Canada. While the obvious cost savings can't be discounted, Kripke says, "*The X-Files* was the main reason for the move." Along with numerous other genre shows shot in Vancouver — like *Dark Angel*, *Smallville*, and *Stargate SG-1* — *The X-Files* is well-known for putting British Columbia's diverse geography to good use. "I originally thought it'd be shot in southern California and maintain that dusty Route 66 look, but there's very few images in that pilot that couldn't have been shot up north." As set decorator George Neuman puts it, "They're fighting evil, and evil doesn't necessarily live in a bright cheery home in Santa Monica Beach."

Producer Cyrus Yavneh explains how they've overcome the separation from the

DID YOU KNOW?

In one of many versions of the pilot script, Sam suspected Dean of being a serial killer, and of murdering their father!

executive producers. "Everything — from wardrobe to the color of a car to casting to location pictures to any number of design and logistic aspects — goes online and is sent to LA, who immediately respond."

Kripke can't say enough about how much he loves the Vancouver team. "They're the best I've ever worked with, and we're all a family — that's what makes it so special." As one of many examples, he points out how well director of photography Serge Ladouceur took his initial cues from 'The Pilot' and has proceeded to make the show so distinctly his own. "He has to manage the same level of quality Aaron achieved on half the time and with half the money. We have a real burden in that the show has to look like a movie every week... and we wouldn't be able to do it without Serge.

"And as much as I love [property master] Scotty Nifong and the work he did [on 'The Pilot'], Chris Cooper is doing an unbelievable job in props week in and week out, maintaining that blue-collar look and feel, and again for half the time and half the money. Likewise, Mike Novotny did such a tremendous job designing 'The Pilot', but Jerry Wanek, who is designing the series, is unbelievable. How that guy can even come up with the amount of motel rooms he comes up with, blows my mind. He and his team are such geniuses, and move with such speed and so little money, that you'd never feel like the sets you were watching have only been there for seventy-two hours. The fact that he's able to accomplish what he accomplishes is a minor miracle every week."

Production manager George Grieve says he would "take this crew on any project. What I find is different with this show is there's a hundred percent respect throughout... and that's a big thing, because I've worked on a lot of shows where that didn't exist — and the people within it weren't as happy."

Ackles is also full of praise for "the brilliance of the people involved," both in Vancouver and Burbank, "from the writing to production. It's not an easy genre to really get. It's challenging to all of us to really make that a scary show every week."

Kripke hopes to be making scary shows for many weeks and years to come. "When we began season one, we had the first two seasons mapped out in terms of where we wanted things to go and the big milestones we wanted to hit." The supply of urban legends and American folklore is so deep, the show could go on indefinitely. And while Kripke is in no hurry to reach the series finale, the overall arc has been envisioned. "We know what the last batch of episodes is going to be... what the endgame looks like... what the final frame of film looks like... We know how Sam and Dean end things."

One thing is for sure, the end will be as exciting as what began on September 13, 2005. ✐

TAG, YOU'RE DEAD

Eric Kripke always wanted the tagline for *Supernatural* to be 'No Rest For the Wicked', but the network wasn't into that. Instead, he went with '*Star Wars* in Truck Stop America'. After all, who wouldn't want to watch Han Solo and Luke Skywalker with chainsaws in the trunk?

THE EPISODES

DEAN: I can't do this alone.
SAM: Yes, you can.
DEAN: Yeah, well I don't want to.

SEASON 1 REGULAR CAST:

Main
Jared Padalecki (Sam Winchester)
Jensen Ackles (Dean Winchester)

Recurring
Jeffrey Dean Morgan (John Winchester)
Samantha Smith (Mary Winchester)
Nicki Aycox (Meg Masters)

THE PILOT

Written by:
Eric Kripke

Directed by:
David Nutter

Guest Cast: Sarah Shahi (Constance Welch), Hunter Brochu (Young Dean), Ross Kohn (Troy Squire), Elizabeth Bond (Amy), R.D. Call (Sheriff Pierce), Derek Webster (Deputy Jaffe), Robert Peters (Deputy Hein), Jamil Z. Smith (Luis), Cletus Young (Motel Clerk), Rick Dano (Deputy Swartz), Steve Railsback (Joseph Welch), Adrianne Palicki (Jessica), Miriam Korn (Rachel), Alex A.J. Rassamni (Constance's Son), Kaitlin Claire Machina (Constance's Daughter)

Twenty-three years ago, in Lawrence, Kansas, the violent, paranormal death of Mary Winchester forever altered the lives of her loving husband, John, her young son, Dean, and her baby, Sam. Dragged across the country from motel to motel by a distraught father hell-bent on revenge, the children grew up trained to hunt and fight supernatural monsters. Yet, they never found the demon that killed their mother, and as soon as he could, Sam escaped to college to start a "normal" life...

Sam is close to graduating from Stanford University when Dean, who he hasn't seen since he left for college, shows up in the middle of the night and insists he help find their father, who has gone missing. Sam is reluctant to leave his new life and his girlfriend, Jessica, but reluctantly agrees to go on the condition that Dean gets him back in time for an interview he has lined up with a prestigious law school.

They travel to their father's last known location, the small town of Jericho, California, where they discover that men are being lured to their deaths by a mysterious Woman in White. From clues left in their father's journal and his abandoned motel room, they figure out that the killer preying on unfaithful men is the spirit of a woman who killed her own children after finding out her husband committed adultery. The brothers become separated when Dean is arrested for impersonating a federal agent, and Sam literally drives right into the ghost. But when Sam doesn't fall under her seductive spell, the angry spirit attacks him despite his faithfulness. Dean escapes and arrives just in time to distract the ghost long enough for Sam to take her home, where the spirits of her children pull her into the afterlife.

Sam returns to Stanford, where he witnesses Jessica's death, caused by the same fiery force that claimed his mother.

SAM: When I told dad I was scared of the thing in my closet he gave me a .45.
DEAN: Well, what was he supposed to do?
SAM: I was nine years old. He was supposed to say, "Don't be afraid of the dark."
DEAN: Don't be afraid of the dark? What, are you kidding me? Of course you should be afraid of the dark! You know what's out there!

DID YOU KNOW?

Every street referenced in 'The Pilot' is a real street in Toledo, Ohio, Eric Kripke's home town.

MUSIC

'Gasoline'
by The Living Daylights
'What Cha Gonna Do'
by Classic
'Speaking In Tongues'
by Eagles Of Death
Metal
'Ramblin' Man'
by The Allman Brothers
'Back In Black'
by AC/DC
'Highway To Hell'
by AC/DC
'My Cheatin' Ways'
by Kid Gloves Music

"Our mission was to make a movie and we did," producer Cyrus Yavneh proclaims. "I love 'The Pilot'!"

Director David Nutter would be happy to hear that. "My attitude is always that I have to fall in love with it before someone else does. For the pilot you're the one creating the look, casting the characters. I used a great guy in Vancouver by the name of Adrien van Viersen, a storyboard artist. You get a chance to figure out some of the big sequences and how best to portray those important sequences." Nutter "really knows the craft," van Viersen notes. "He's the most visual director I've worked with."

One of the first scenes van Viersen storyboarded was the potent visual of an ablaze Mary Winchester pinned to the ceiling. Actress Samantha Smith recalls the real flames all too well. "It was a little freaky. There were two long fires — from propane pipes — on either side of me. They were probably five feet away from me on either side, and I was lying on the ground. I wasn't in any hurry to stand up and move until they'd turned them off! And then we had a fake person on a fake ceiling and they lit it up, and the room actually caught on fire really fast and they had to evacuate."

"The fire laughs," sound supervisor Mike Lawshe discloses. "It actually has some very strange croaking sounds that go along with it so that you know that's not just fire, there's something causing it from the other side."

What's the best way to fight hellfire? Chances are the answer can be found in John Winchester's journal or the trunk of Dean's inherited Impala. "These things that are really anthemic to the show were created by Scotty [Nifong]," executive producer Eric Kripke says. "The way we described the trunk in the script was it was a trunk full of weapons, some blue-collar, and some mysterious and occult-like. Any weapon you can think of, any object you can think of, any tool you can think of — you basically have this magic box in the back of the car that you can reach in and pull out anything. The aesthetic of the show is greasy and dirty. It isn't about magic wands or magic amulets. You had to have crowbars and power drills, but then also this bizarre knife that you've never seen before... and a spear gun! It was everybody's instinct at first to make them too neat and clean, like James Bond. I want stuff that they had to nail together and jerry rig themselves."

Kripke says that the journal is "very visually interesting with densely packed writing," but he'll never let the viewers "get close enough to the book to read the text of what it says about the creatures."

P.19
Sam and Dean examine the clues their father left behind.
Opposite
John Winchester cries out in horror at the sight of his dying wife.

OFFICER: So, fake U.S. Marshall. Fake credit cards. You got anything that's real?
DEAN: My boobs.

The scene right before the trunk is first opened, where the brothers discuss how they were raised, was a trouble spot for Kripke. "The music that they'd gotten in there before felt too sappy to him," composer Christopher Lennertz says. "He told me it should be in the world of scary and supernatural, it should never be so schmaltzy. I probably wrote four or five versions of that cue... and eventually it got much more towards scary and had a little bit of the emotions and tried to be a hybrid."

The other important musical moment in 'The Pilot', Lennertz asserts, comes in just before the demon shows up to take first Mary and later Jess. "We set the tone for this motif that was a very dissonant solo piano with a lot of reverb on it, a lot of echo that sounded really nasty. In the midst of this cacophony, suddenly everything would drop away and it would be this clanky, nasty, twentieth-century kind of piano thing that sounded wrong to the ear.

"'The Pilot' set the tone for the entire show." ✍

BEING SAM

When asked what he brings to his character, Jared Padalecki says, "great looks" without missing a beat. Despite the humorous remark, the actor is truly modest and has always been self-conscious of what he brings to the role, particularly in 'The Pilot'. "I watch it and I'm like, 'Ugh, why'd they hire me?' But for 'Wendigo', I watched it and there's a part where we're sitting by the campfire and I was like, 'Ah, cool, I'm proud of that.' That was a step toward where I wanted to be. A lot of the interactions that Jensen, Jeff, and I had I felt good about, I felt like I was in the moment and I was Sam. But so often I felt kind of searching, but maybe that's in character, 'cause Sam's kind of searching, and Sam is kind of lost, and Sam doesn't know what he's doing or why he's doing what he's doing. So maybe life imitates art — maybe that's just the dialogue rubbing off on me or something."

DID YOU KNOW?

Eric Kripke and David Nutter worked together previously on the Warner Bros. TV series *Tarzan*.

WENDIGO

Written by:
Eric Kripke and
Ron Milbauer &
Terri Hughes
Burton

Directed by:
David Nutter

Guest Cast: Roy Campsall (Wendigo), Alden Ehrenreich (Ben Collins), Gina Holden (Haley Collins), Cory Monteith (Gary), Callum Keith Rennie (Roy), Donnelly Rhodes (Stevenson Shaw), Graham Wardle (Tommy Collins), Timothy Webber (Park Ranger Wilkinson), Rhys Williams (Brad), Wren Robertz (Tough Local), Tamara Lashley (Paramedic), Roy Campsall

am and Dean follow the coordinates left in their father's journal to Blackwater Ridge, Lost Creek, Colorado, where they learn that some campers have gone missing. They pose as park rangers to talk to Haley Collins, who has lost contact with her brother, Tommy. She gives them a video message Tommy sent, and when Sam plays it frame by frame they discover something ominous: the shadow of a large creature can be seen outside Tommy's tent.

Research reveals that people have been vanishing in the area every twenty-three years since at least 1936, supposedly victims of grizzly bear attacks. The brothers speak with a survivor of a 1959 attack, Shaw, who confirms their suspicions of supernatural involvement when he swears "some kind of *demon*" took his parents.

Sam and Dean join Haley and her younger brother, Ben, and follow a professional guide, Roy, into the woods to find Tommy. They soon determine that they are dealing with a wendigo, a former human whose cannibalism has transformed him into a creature with superhuman strength and speed. When they realize that their father was never in Blackwater Ridge, and that he sent them there to kill the wendigo, Dean convinces Sam to embrace the family business of hunting evil things and saving people. Roy scoffs at the brothers' warnings and gets himself killed. The wendigo captures Dean and Haley, but they are quickly rescued by Sam and Ben. Dean then offers himself up as bait so that the others, along with Tommy (the sole surviving camper), can escape. Dean knows he can't kill a wendigo with bullets or knifes, so he uses a flare gun to destroy the beast.

SAM: We cannot let that Haley girl go out there.
DEAN: Oh, yeah? What are we gonna tell her? She can't go into the woods because of a big, scary monster?
SAM: Yeah.

With the show's move from Los Angeles to Vancouver, David Nutter was asked to stay on and direct the first episode. He had to "start with a whole new group of people and get them excited about the series. So in a sense it's doing another pilot for half the time and half the money," comments Nutter. "It was a real tough experience, but Cyrus Yavneh put together a great crew with George Grieve in Vancouver, and Bob Singer, and it just worked out perfectly."

DID YOU KNOW?

The composer for this episode, Jay Gruska, was also the composer for 'The Wendigo' episode of fellow WB show, *Charmed*, a supernatural-themed series with all-female leads. That show's portrayal of the wendigo creature, however, borrowed heavily from werewolf lore.

Nutter feels the success of the episode's scares are due to the editing. "It's what you didn't see, because the character wasn't all that ferocious. In television, you can't really scare people. I would hearken back to my *X-Files* days, and what you don't see is more scary than what you do see."

Eric Kripke agrees that the wendigo character didn't turn out all that ferocious. "If you look at the final version of 'Wendigo', you almost never see the creature. Believe me, there is a lot more footage of that wendigo front and center that is on the cutting room floor because I just wasn't happy with the way it looked," admits Kripke. "Any creature we create has the burden of having to be realistic. It was really the first rude awakening we — the production staff — had of [the fact that] we don't have as much time and money to execute this as we did on 'The Pilot'," Kripke elaborates. "I thought everyone did a valiant job trying to make the wendigo work, but the wendigo just didn't work. On a TV show schedule you have time to see a drawing, give notes, let them incorporate the notes, maybe give one more round of notes, then that's it, they have to make the creature. And in that case, once we saw the finished product, it wasn't as awe-inspiring and terrifying as we'd hoped it would

Above

Sam puts his life between his new friends and the wendigo.

be, and he looked more like Gollum's tall, gangly cousin than anything else."

Kripke has since learned his lesson: "Don't attempt something you know you can't execute. Limitations are actually very good for creativity because you find creative ways around them. And it's made us better storytellers."

Art director John Marcynuk has a differing view of the wendigo, which is one of his favorite creations from the season. "Although you don't really catch much, there was a lot of thought put into that creature because that was our first episode and we had a little more presence in the design," he explains. "Later on, [the design] was kind of released to a multitude of somewhat successful and somewhat unsuccessful special effects and makeup houses. You had varying degrees of quality and competence. Certainly, for monsters, that one stands out in my mind."

For this episode, the sets the art department designed included a cave and a

MUSIC

'Hot Blooded'
by Foreigner
'Down South Jukin'
by Lynyrd Skynyrd
'Fly By Night'
by Rush

mineshaft for the wendigo to live in — its lair. "Part of it we shot out in a mine in Britannia Beach, and that had its challenges, but a good portion we ended up on stage to do that, because it's really awkward to shoot in such locations." There's also a strong fire element in the ending, when the creature meets its demise, so they had to deal with the fireproofing of the set.

SAM: It's a damn near perfect hunter. It's smarter than you, and it's gonna hunt you down and eat you alive unless we get your stupid, sorry ass out of here.
ROY: You know you're crazy, right?

Visual effects supervisor Ivan Hayden was also involved with the fire component. "At the end they did a practical gag where stunts and special effects set the actor on fire using a flame gel, and he fell to the ground. In post-production they felt that they wanted to draw out the moment a little bit more," Hayden recalls. "The decision came down that it felt a little bit too quick for the tension and buildup of the scene. I got the special effects guys to make a mannequin out of wire-frame, then we took steel wool and wrapped it. And then we ignited it using batteries, and that gives a very distinctive look when steel wool burns — it sorta looks like a cigar element. We then composited that into the wendigo footage and prolonged that main moment of him dying."

Blackwater Ridge Review

October, 1959
YOUNG BOY INCREDIBLY SURVIVES SAVAGE ATTACK

Nine-year-old Stevenson Shaw crawled out of Lost Creek yesterday morning, barely alive. Injured, exhausted, and clearly traumatized, the boy claimed that a monster had dragged his parents off into the night.

The rangers coordinated a search party, but were unable to find any trace of Stevenson's parents, save for the trail of blood that led off into the woods. "That kid's parents got mauled by a grizzly, plain and simple," Ranger Daniels asserted. "Where it took them, I couldn't tell you."

When asked what he saw, the boy trembled as he spoke. "I... I didn't see it — it moved so... so *fast*. It wasn't a bear. That *roar* was unnatural..." Then young Stevenson Shaw looked at me with an intensity this reporter's rarely seen. "How'd it get inside our cabin? It didn't smash a window or break the door. What kind of bear can turn a doorknob?"

I had no answer for him, and I suspect no one ever will.

By Henry Morgan

A Closer Look At:

THE WOMAN IN WHITE

You only have to look as far as the simplest, cheapest, and arguably most popular Halloween costume ever made — a sheet thrown over your head with two eye holes cut out — to be reminded that ghosts are usually depicted as being draped in flowing white garments. What makes the Woman in White memorable is that she is beautiful and haunts roadways.

In the famous urban legend of the Vanishing Hitchhiker, a man gives a mysterious hitchhiker a ride, but upon reaching her requested destination, he turns to say goodbye and discovers she has disappeared from the car. He shrugs it off, as if he had been distracted by something and didn't hear the door as his passenger hurried away… until he later learns his passenger had died quite some time ago. There are various versions of this legend, including ones that involve horses and wagons rather than cars. Some state that the hitchhiker leaves behind an object such as a book or scarf, while in other versions the hitchhiker disappears when the vehicle drives past a graveyard.

Then there's the famous Mexican story about La Llorona (the weeping woman). In this tragic tale set hundreds of years ago, a beautiful Indian princess, Dona Luisa de Loveros, fell in love with a handsome Mexican nobleman, Don Nuno de Montesclaros. The princess loved the nobleman and had two children with him, but he refused to marry her. When he finally left her and married another woman, Dona went into a rage and murdered her children. She was later found wandering the streets in a daze, her clothes covered in blood. She was charged with infanticide and sentenced to death. Ever since, it is said that her ghost wanders the country's roads and waterways, preying on unfaithful men.

SAM: What were you thinking, shooting Casper in the face, you freak?
DEAN: Hey, I saved your ass!

"Both of them are very, very old," Eric Kripke says of the legends that inspired the Woman in White. "I just combined them to create that particular vengeful spirit. The story of the Vanishing Hitchhiker is one of the most well-known urban legends, which is why I wanted to start with it in 'The Pilot'. But to give her more motivation and flesh her out, and give her a little more characterization, we used elements of La Llorona. They say the Vanishing Hitchhiker may have been inspired by La Llorona, so there's actually a cultural connection between them."

A Closer Look At:
WENDIGOS

Different origins of the wendigo exist — including spirit possession and clinical psychosis — but the most widespread lore warns of black magic and cannibalism. The stories have been passed down by Native American tribes, as well as explorers and missionaries across North America from as far back as the seventeenth century. The tales usually involve a harsh winter, and someone being cut off from supplies and resorting to eating his family or friends to survive. Only, he doesn't truly survive, as his evil act turns him into something less than human…

The wendigo — aka the Evil That Devours — is said to be larger than human, emaciated (from its constant hunger), with teeth and fingernails that have grown into fangs and claws, and glowing eyes. This creature, that stalks hunters and campers in dark forests, is known to have inhuman speed and strength.

DEAN: Chow time, you freaky bastard! Yeah, that's right, bring it on, baby. I taste good!

According to Eric Kripke, the inspiration for the look of *Supernatural*'s wendigo creature came from an Aphex Twin music video, 'Come To Daddy', directed by Chris Cunningham. "There's this creature in it that kinda rises up and it's got this huge mouth with these big, big teeth, and it's sorta pale and bald, and it opens up its mouth unnaturally wide and screams right in the face of this old woman, and her hair is all blown back. That was the conception for the wendigo," reveals Kripke. "Wendigos started out human, so we wanted it to have human features. We trotted out this video and showed it to everybody and said, 'This is what we want to accomplish.' It's a really disturbing creature in that video."

A logical extension of the wendigo once being human is its ability to imitate human voices, which is not a trait commonly associated with the wendigo myth, but it's an idea that the show used to creepy effect.

Perhaps the most important thing to know about wendigos is how to kill them. As with many other supernatural monsters, a silver bullet (or silver arrowhead) to the heart is rumoured to do the trick. However, in most lore, during the transformation from human to wendigo, the creature's heart turns to solid ice… so a silver or lead ice pick to the heart should work too. But the only way to be sure a wendigo is dead and gone is to set it on fire and watch its icy heart melt.

DEAD IN THE WATER

Written by:
Raelle Tucker,
Sera Gamble
Directed by:
Kim Manners

Guest Cast: Amber Borycki (Sophie Carlton), Amy Acker (Andrea Barr), Keira Kabatow (Waitress), Bruce Dawson (Bill Carlton), Aaron Rota, Troy Clare, D. Harlan Cutshall, Nico McEown (Lucas Barr), Daniel Hugh Kelly (Sheriff Jake Devins), Bethoe Shirkoff

When the trail for their father goes cold, Dean scans the news headlines for mysterious occurrences. When he discovers that Sophie Carlton is the third Lake Manitoc drowning in the past year — and that all of the bodies have disappeared, despite the lake being dragged — he convinces Sam that they should go to Wisconsin to investigate.

Pretending they were sent by the Federal Wildlife Service to investigate the possibility of a natural predator in the lake area, the brothers visit the sheriff for answers. They meet the sheriff's pretty daughter, Andrea, and mute grandson, Luke, and learn that the child witnessed his father's death at the lake and hasn't spoken a word since. Dean's charm doesn't entirely win Andrea over, but he makes a connection with the boy, who draws him a picture of the Carlton home.

By the time Sam and Dean determine that the lake is haunted by the spirit of a boy accidentally killed by the sheriff and Sophie's father when they were all kids, the entire Carlton family has been murdered. The vengeful ghost goes after Andrea next, but the brothers rescue her from drowning in her bathtub. The problem is, the child's body was never recovered, so there are no bones for the brothers to salt and burn. The lonely ghost lures Lucas to the lake and Dean rescues him, but only after the grief-stricken sheriff sacrifices himself to appease the ghost and protect his family.

ANDREA: Must be hard, with your sense of direction, never being able to find your way to a decent pick-up line.

"I kind of always stuck to 'Dead in the Water' being one of my favorites," Jensen Ackles reveals. "It really helped me get an understanding on Dean from the different levels I got to play in that particular episode. And it was the first episode we did with Kim [Manners] — it kind of gave us Kim, so that was a nice thing."

The episode also gave genre fans a taste of Amy Acker in a "good girl" role after the nastier characters she'd recently played on *Alias* and *Angel*. In her memorable bathtub scene, Amy was covered in brown goo, which she described as "like a day at the spa" because of the chocolate milk utilized in the mix. "Everybody seemed to like me better — I guess they thought I was really sweet," Acker giggles.

Ackles was worried that she wouldn't be sweet, seeing as how the two Texans went to rival high schools. "I went to LV Berkner High School and she went to Lake

Above
Sheriff Jake Devins
deep in thought at the
Lake Manitoc crime
scene.

Highlands High School," Ackles explains. "We were bitter rivals, for sure. When I found out she was a Wildcat, I was like, 'Ah, we're not going to get along at all!' And we didn't — it was fist fights every day. No, but we did, and she's a lovely person, and that was another reason I love 'Dead in the Water' so much, because of Amy — she was awesome."

"We were in Canada, but it felt like I was back home," Acker says. "I had such a great time." She'd be happy to work on the show again, but she's not sure there's a place for Andrea in Dean's life. "It seemed like it would have been a perfect thing to have a romance with him. At first I thought maybe it meant something that he was attracted to me, like I was special, and then I watched a couple more episodes and I was, 'Oh, I don't think he likes me very much...'"

The only thing Ackles didn't like about that episode was when he had to hold his breath while holding Nico McEown, who played Lucas, in his arms. "We had to literally get pulled down by divers underneath the water and held underwater about ten feet," he recalls. "That's a scary feeling, especially when you're holding a ten-year-old boy in your arms and he's pretending to be lifeless. Luckily, we got through it and it's all good."

Acker appreciated the way that scene was filmed. "I thought that was a neat directorial choice, how [Kim Manners] slowed down the camera and took out all the

sound when Jared and Jensen were looking for my son."

Costume designer Diane Widas found that scene challenging. "We had a little boy who had to be in lake water for a long time, so we had to develop the costume to be able to go over the wet suit. And because his clothing was really deteriorated and holey, wherever there were holes, the special effects makeup people had to vein the wet suit." She points out that Ackles and Padalecki needed to jump in the lake with their clothes on too. "We had to be careful to not pick something that would be hard to swim in and put them in jeopardy."

DEAN: I just don't want to leave this town until I know the kid's okay.
SAM: Who are you? And what have you done with my brother?
DEAN: Shut up.

"There were all kinds of interesting challenges," director Kim Manners recalls. "We were supposed to blow up a boat, blow it out of the water with a guy in it. We were originally going to do that practically, but it proved impractical to do it practically, so we did it CGI. We had a lot of underwater photography in a very cold lake. It was a tough show, but it came out really well."

"The learning curve was huge," writer Sera Gamble admits, referring to how she'd "never written pure horror." Her writing partner, Raelle Tucker, agrees. "I remember the first time we had this dead boy in the water, we gave him like five-hundred powers. It took us a while to really understand how to ground these characters and make them believable. And we were asking, 'Did we make a mistake? Are we on the wrong show? We suck at this!' But it got better. I actually think it came to life on the screen because the water is so incredible. Kim Manners did an excellent job of shooting it, and you're afraid of water. I wish I could take credit for this, but this is Bob Singer's idea: when the guy drowns in the kitchen sink. That's when it crosses the line. It's not *Jaws*, it's not just creeping up on you under the water — it's like, you can't take a bath, you can't wash the dishes, it's any water. That was awesome." ✍

Opposite

Dean and Sam pose as agents of the Federal Wildlife Service.

Below

Sam and Dean get a closer look at the deadly Lake Manitoc.

PHANTOM TRAVELER

Written by:
Richard Hatem

Directed by:
Robert Singer

Guest Cast: Kelly-Ruth Mercier (Woman Passenger), Geoff Gustafson (Lou), Benjamin Ayres (Homeland Security Man), Dana Pemberton (Guard), Ingrid Tesch (Bonnie Phelps), Amanda Wood (Flight Attendant), Christopher Rosamund (Co-Pilot), Fred Henderson (Man), Paul Jarrett (George Phelps), Jaime Ray Newman (Amanda Walker), Kett Turton (Max Jaffe), Daryl Shuttleworth (Captain Chuck Lambert), Brian Markinson (Jerry Panowski)

Dean gets a call from Jerry Panowski, a man he and his father had once saved from a poltergeist. Jerry is the lead mechanic for United Britannia Airlines, and one of their planes went down under mysterious circumstances. The brothers agree to join him at Pittsburgh International Airport.

There were seven survivors, including the pilot and a stewardess named Amanda, but when they go over the flight recording, they hear the ominous warning, "No survivors." They talk to a survivor who checked himself into a psychiatric facility, and the man tells them he saw a passenger with black eyes open the plane's pressure-sealed hatch. Next they talk to the widow of the man who caused the crash, and leave with the impression that he was likely possessed. After donning cheap black suits and flashing forged Homeland Security badges, Sam and Dean examine the wreckage, where they find some sulphuric residue that confirms their suspicions of demonic activity. The surviving pilot is possessed by the demon and crashes a small plane.

Sam and Dean know they must exorcise the demon before it attacks the remaining survivors, but when they fail to stop Amanda from boarding another plane, the brothers realize the only way to save her is to take the battle to the skies. Trouble is, Dean has a bit of a problem with flying... He conquers his fears, and once aboard the plane learns that this flight's co-pilot is now possessed. He manages to convince Amanda to bring the co-pilot to him, and he and Sam perform an exorcism. The demon boasts he knows what happened to Sam's girlfriend, but they continue with the ritual and although the plane nearly crashes, they finish the ritual and touch down safely.

SAM: Look, I appreciate your concern —
DEAN: Oh, I'm not concerned about _you_. It's your job to keep my ass alive! So I need you sharp.

"I really liked 'Phantom Traveler', supervising producer Phil Sgriccia exclaims. "You're in a haunted house, but you can't leave the haunted house because you're 35,000 feet above the earth. So it was a bit like _Alien_ in that respect because you're on this plane with this monster thing and you can't leave."

DID YOU KNOW?

For a time, if you called Dean's cell number, 866-907-3235, you'd hear Jensen Ackles reading the message: "This is Dean Winchester. If this is an emergency, please leave a message. If you are calling about 11-2-83, page me with your coordinates." 11/2/83 is the date of Mary Winchester's death.

Executive producer Robert Singer was not scheduled to direct this episode, but he's glad he did. "The director, for whatever reason, had to bail out at the last minute," he explains. "I liked that script a lot. That it set into everyone's fear of the plane going down. There was a lot of humor in that one, which I enjoyed doing, and Jensen was great. It was revealing of the character — we learned that this guy that we've seen for three episodes prior to that, who seemed to be fearless, had this Achilles heel, he's afraid to fly. That put another layer on it. That one was a lot of fun to do.

"I think we got out of the gate, like a lot of series do, with a few fits and starts," Singer maintains. "I think once we did 'Phantom Traveler', things started to fall in place really well." Production designer Jerry Wanek supports that opinion. "'Phantom Traveler' was the first time that I felt the brothers really started connecting and were totally believable. That was a big thing for the show in general."

This episode was memorable for costume designer Diane Widas since "That was the first time we used the black suits. Because these guys are who they are, a real generic guy's suit is what they have. They were ill-fitting, a little short... but that was the plan, so that they were a little bit off, so that they don't look like the real [Homeland Security agents] when you see them later." Widas also recalls the need to make multiples of the co-pilot's clothes because the "special effects guys had to throw holy water on the fellow and make him burn. We had to build special apparatus for

Above

Dean spots the demon-possessed co-pilot.

underneath so that the actor was protected but it would still work on the costume, and the rest of the costume wouldn't go up in flames."

"'Phantom Traveler' was a challenging episode for us," says set decorator George Neuman. "We had to reconstruct an airplane after a crash. It was very challenging just to put this thing together on such a large scale. And to do it in such a short period of time amongst all the other sets that we're continually doing... It was a very nice shot, but on the episode you couldn't really tell how enormous that actual set was." Art director John Marcynuk also remembers the unusual production challenge. "We dragged in a bunch of airplane parts from various sources to create a reconstruction of an aircraft. That was interesting, working in an airport hanger, laying out a graphic of a plane on the ground and building up from there."

SAM: What is that?
DEAN: It's an EMF meter. It reads electromagnetic frequencies.
SAM: Yeah, I know what an EMF meter is — but why does that one look like a busted-up walkman?
DEAN: Because that's what I made it out of.

"'Phantom Traveler' was a tough one for us," admits visual effects supervisor Ivan Hayden. "All the airplane stuff we built on computers, every single shot. None of it existed. Anytime you saw an airplane outside, we had to do it — we had to get background plates and CG clouds, we had to model the airplanes, texture them, and light them." Not that it was all a chore. "Doing the demon smoke and having the guy get sucked out of the airplane was a lot of fun. It was a really good episode and we

MUSIC

'Paranoid'
by Black Sabbath
'Working Man'
by Rush
'Load Rage'
by Nichion Sounds
Library

were really pleased with how it turned out. I think the worst comment I had, I read on the internet where someone said it looked like a miniature, and we were like, 'Yes! It looked real — it looked like a miniature, but it looked real!'"

The "real" EMF meter was designed and made by Chris Coopers' prop department, and he promises it is actually made out of an old walkman. "We have the EMF detector that they use all the time. It has an analog meter on it, and then some LED lights that go up and down to make it look like things are going on. Actually, I can't let out the secrets of how it all works…" ✦

Below

Demon-possessed passenger George Phelps makes an emergency exit.

the evil that devours — silver. vengeful lake/water. child?

FLIGHT 401. CRASHED INTO FLORIDA SWAMP. SALVAGED PARTS PUT INTO OTHER PLANES
PILOT BOB LOFT / COPILOT DON REPO — HAUNTING FLIGHTS? ID'ED FROM PHOTOGRAPHS BY
PASSENGERS — WITNESSES OR JUST FOAF?
DEMONIC POSSESSION???

Mirrors. bleeding eyes

BLOODY MARY

Written by:
Terri Hughes
Burton, Ron
Milbauer

Directed by:
Peter Ellis

Guest Cast: Jovanna Huguet (Bloody Mary/Mary Worthington), Michael Teigen (Teacher), Victoria Tennant, Jessica King, Duncan Minett (Steven Shoemaker), James Ashcroft (Coroner), Genevieve Buechner (Lily Shoemaker), Kristie Marsden (Donna Shoemaker), William Taylor (Detective Jackson Riley), Marnette Patterson (Charlie), Adrianne Palicki (Jessica Moore), Chelan Simmons (Jill)

In Toledo, Ohio, a group of twelve-year-old girls dare Lily Shoemaker to look into her bathroom mirror and repeat "Bloody Mary" three times. This unleashes a specter that murders Lily's father, which Dean reads about and decides to investigate. He rouses Sam from a nightmare about Jessica once they reach the morgue. Sam bribes a morgue tech with Dean's hard-earned poker money, and they learn that Steven Shoemaker's eyeballs practically exploded. They go to Shoemaker's home, where they are able to slip in among the mourners. Lily tells them what happened, and her older sister, Donna, ridicules her, but her friend Charlie is spooked. On her way home, Charlie talks to her friend Jill, who jokingly calls out to Bloody Mary while still on the phone. She fakes dying, but then falls prey to Mary for real.

Despite Jill dying in the same manner as her father, Donna won't listen, and she spitefully chants "Bloody Mary" while she and Charlie stand in front of a mirror. Mary stalks Charlie through a variety of reflective surfaces, and the terrified girl calls the brothers for help. Sam and Dean uncover the source of the original legend — an unsolved murder of a woman who died in front of a mirror — and track down her mirror to a local antique store. Sam summons Mary into her mirror, but guilt over Jessica's death allows Mary to make his eyes bleed. Dean comes to his aid, but when they smash Mary's mirror, the phantom crawls out of it. With his eyes bleeding, Dean shoves a mirror in front of Mary's face, and her hatred of people with violent secrets is reflected back on her, causing the spirit to dissolve.

DID YOU KNOW?

The "glass" that Jovanna Huguet's Bloody Mary crawls across is made of rubber. And many of the mirrors that were broken were candy glass, which is made out of sugar — you can eat them!

SAM: Might not be one of ours. Might just be some freak medical thing.
DEAN: How many times in dad's long and varied career has it actually been a freak medical thing and not some sign of an awful supernatural death?
SAM: Uh... Almost never.
DEAN: Exactly.

"I really loved the monster in the mirror behind you," enthuses Eric Kripke. "I thought that was really scary. We ended up making the mistake of making her look too much like the girl in *The Ring*." However, visual effects supervisor Ivan Hayden

Above

Dean takes a whack at Bloody Mary's mirror.

doesn't feel they made a mistake. "We did talk about speed ramping her and having her come out that way, but a lot of TV pays homage to the greats, so if it's something people are liking, give them what they like…" (Speed ramping involves changing the capture frame rate of a camera while filming a scene so a time-manipulation effect is achieved in playback.)

With regards to Dean's eyes bleeding, Kripke says, "There is something in his past — we've always known it. It's been in the core of the character from the time we created him. We will reveal it, but I doubt I'll ever reference 'Bloody Mary' again. We're trying very hard to create a show that once you learn all the secrets, when all is said and done, you can go back over all the episodes and say, 'Oh yeah, they said that…' People think I'm making up what the reason is, but I'm telling you I know."

"'Bloody Mary' was another busy episode for us," art director John Marcynuk recalls. "We had to design a corridor specially so that you don't see the camera as you're tracking with an individual down the corridor because she's reflected in a number of mirrors. We tried to do that as practical as possible. We also created a set where basically it was a refection of a bathroom and we created a whole other reflection of the bathroom and used essentially a twin, so that they were mimicking each other's movements in the mirror. It worked to a certain degree, but I think they ran out of time shooting it to really make it what it could've been."

"Jovanna [Huguet] was great, she was really incredible to work with. And her body movements were really good, just really jerky," key hairstylist Jeannie Chow

DID YOU KNOW?

The episode is set in Eric Kripke's home town, and several of the names mentioned in the dialogue refer to Kripke's good friends.

Above

Sam awaits Bloody Mary's appearance.

MUSIC

'Laugh, I Nearly Died'
by Rolling Stones
'Rock of Ages'
by Def Leppard
'Sugar, We're Going Down'
by Fall Out Boy

recalls. "The Bloody Mary character was just really scary... Even now I can't go into a dark bathroom... But that was a really good transformation. She had shoulder-length hair and I put hair extensions on her to give her that greasy, textured, can't-see-her-face kind of look."

Costume designer Diane Widas put that same greasy texture into Bloody Mary's clothes. "Her costume was a dress that I designed and we made, then we seriously aged it and broke it down and put wax on it and made it look like she was there for a hundred years."

The thing key makeup artist Shannon Coppin remembers the most about this episode was that she worked in conjunction with the special effects team "to match the blood, because when you have a blood rig, there's no way of knowing which way the blood's gonna run and so we would have to match it if it got in her hair or on her costume. Quite often what we'll do is, if there's a special effects makeup, we'll do the whole body and the face and they'll apply the prosthetic, send them back to us, and then we'll make up the difference — we'll try to get rid of the edges and things like that. That was a pretty tricky gag to have. Especially for Jared, who had such short turnarounds as it is, to have a prosthetic like that, which took so long to put on and have him bleeding from his eyes… He's a great guy, but he hates sitting still — for him to sit still for two-and-a-half to three hours, it's just prison."

CHARLIE: I'm insane, right?
DEAN: No, you're not insane.
CHARLIE: God, that makes me feel so much worse!

"The score was really well done at accenting the spook factor," music editor Dino Moriano comments. And composer Christopher Lennertz points out that he knows "Eric really liked the way that score came out. In the glimpses and insinuations [of Bloody Mary] we actually got simpler with the music and we came down to single-string lines that would weave in and out. I don't have to show off in this kind of a section; I don't have to make it really loud and crunchy. I can make these sections really soft and super, super subtle, and it actually makes it scarier."

"Bloody 'Bloody Mary'," sighs set decorator George Neuman. "What I remember about that is buying every mirror in town in triples or quadruples. And they had to be very large mirrors. I remember probably half my budget was spent on the mirrors. And we tried to find enormous, very ornate mirrors. I had buyers driving around all over the place, from shop to shop. Mirrors! That's all I remember. And they all got broken…"

Below
The brothers support each other in the battle against Bloody Mary.

SKIN

Written by:
John Shiban

Directed by:
Robert Duncan
McNeill

Guest Cast: Amy Grabow (Rebecca Warren), Aleks Holtz (Zachary Warren), Shiraine Haas (Jogger), Marrett Green (Newscaster), Anita Brown (Lindsay), Peter Shinkoda (Alex), Ron Blecker (SWAT Captain), Nick Allen (SWAT Teamer)

Sam and Dean rush to the aid of Sam's old college buddy, Zach, who is accused of a murder he swears he didn't commit. Zach's sister, Rebecca, is his alibi, but Dean is a little dubious when Rebecca presents a videotape of someone who resembles Zach entering the victim's home just before the time of the murder. Sam insists Zach is innocent, and Dean starts to come around. They go to the scene of the crime and note that the neighbor's dog went psycho right around when Zach's girlfriend was killed, which is a telltale sign of paranormal activity.

When another murder occurs, the brothers discover a shapeshifter is adopting the likenesses of others. They discover its underground lair, but the hunters become the hunted when the shapeshifter gets the drop on them. The shapeshifter morphs into Dean and uses a psychic connection to "download" Dean's memories. Leaving the brothers tied up in his lair, shapeshifter-Dean pays Rebecca a visit with the hope of igniting some sparks that had passed between her and Dean. But shapeshifter-Dean's own personality colors his interpretation of what Dean would say in a romantic situation and he's rejected by a disgusted Rebecca. So, he tries to kill her. Meanwhile, Sam and Dean have escaped. They call the police, who arrive in time to save Rebecca, but now Dean is a wanted man.

After the police leave, Dean visits Rebecca to ensure she knows it wasn't him earlier, and Sam goes back to the lair. Sam finds Rebecca tied up in the sewers at the same time that shapeshifter-Rebecca gets the jump on Dean and switches back into his skin. Sam races back and has a knock-down-drag-out fight with his brother's doppelganger. The elder brother gets the upper hand and shapeshifter-Dean is about to strangle Sam when the real Dean shoots "himself" dead.

DID YOU KNOW?

'Skin' director Robert Duncan McNeill also directed the episode 'Shots' of the TV series *Eyes*, which was written by *Supernatural* writer and story editor Sera Gamble.

DEAN: Hey. Remember when I said this wasn't our kind of problem?
SAM: Yeah.
DEAN: Definitely our kind of problem.

"We first started to catch our vibe with 'Skin'," Eric Kripke asserts. "I loved 'Bloody Mary' and I loved 'Phantom Traveler', but they're fun and just about the monster concept. 'Skin' was the first time we started to dig deeper, the first episode that we really started to feel like, 'Oh, well hey, there's actually more interesting levels here than just the scares. Jensen got to be evil. He got to say things that his character

might be too reserved to say, or too repressed to say."

"It was a really enjoyable show for me to watch," says Jared Padalecki. "I remember I enjoyed filming it. We had that fight scene that took all day to film. Ten... fifteen seconds long. Everything just came together, and I loved the dynamic of these brothers clashing."

According to stunt coordinator Lou Bollo, that was "one of the most difficult

Above

Dean and Sam examine some "puke-inducing" skin.

MUSIC

'In-A-Gadda-Da-Vida'
by Iron Butterfly
'Poison Whiskey'
by Lynyrd Skynyrd
'Hey Man, Nice Shot'
by Filter
'All Right Now'
by Free

sequences we did. It was a scene where the two brothers had to face off. They had to do a fight in a games room, and I remember the producers coming to me and saying, 'Look, you're gonna have to work with these guys over the weekend for two days to get this fight down, because it's a very long, brutal fight that's going to feature a lot of the guys, with stunt doubles of course.' Having worked with them already, I knew this wasn't going to be two days, because they are *so* quick at picking up stuff. We literally had it done in four hours. We got a call from *Kung Fu* magazine, who wanted to do an interview about that particular fight. The main engines behind that fight were Jared and Jensen, because without their physical ability you couldn't possibly do it. It's because these guys are so precise and so smart about what they do that it just came off without a hitch."

Editor Anthony Pinker notes that "with the exception of the guy going into the bookshelf and then falling into the coffee table," he used cuts with Ackles and

Padalecki. "I was supposed to just use them for close-ups, or whatever, and I was telling Phil [Sgriccia], 'These guys are good. I don't see any reason to do trickery here with the editing because they're really good.'"

Opposite
Rebecca Warren finds herself in a bind.

Location manager Russ Hamilton thinks 'Skin' is one of the best episodes they produced in season one. "Largely because of the set design — I thought the set design was absolutely amazing."

DEAN: I think we're close to its lair...
SAM: Why do you say that?
DEAN: Because there's another puke-inducing pile next to your face...

"I gotta say my favorite [season one] episode was 'Skin'," claims co-executive producer John Shiban. "Not just because I wrote it and it was well-executed... It really worked as a thriller, a great supernatural mystery. And I think the director did a phenomenal job with it.

"If you're doing a shapeshifting episode, he has to shapeshift into one of our guys. He just has to," Shiban insists. "The problem becomes, if he's a bad guy and he's walking around as Dean, then how do you clear Dean at the end of it? We wrestled with that. And it can be scary, because you're wondering, is this gonna just destroy the series? Are we going to find ourselves in three weeks going, 'Why the hell did we do that?' I think ultimately, in the long run, it was a great layer to add to the characters and it's led to new characters and new situations where you go, 'Remember that? Well, now we can use that in this episode.' He can't go to the police now because his name will show up. Or even just something small like in 'The Benders' where Dean's looking for Sam under an alias and Dean hears about his own reputation, which is a nice little moment. And you can't deny that it happened — once you shoot it and it airs, it's part of the canon, it's part of the show. But that's what makes it exciting in a way."

"I love where the doppelganger tears the skin off," producer Cyrus Yavneh proclaims. "I did the inserts of the teeth and the ears, and the ripping off and the teeth falling out, so that was a lot of fun. I grossed everybody out and they loved it. I loved that episode just because of how weird and strange it was." 🖋

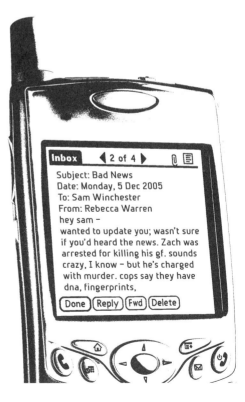

Inbox ◀ 2 of 4 ▶

Subject: Bad News
Date: Monday, 5 Dec 2005
To: Sam Winchester
From: Rebecca Warren
hey sam –
wanted to update you; wasn't sure if you'd heard the news. Zach was arrested for killing his gf. sounds crazy, I know – but he's charged with murder. cops say they have dna, fingerprints,

Done Reply Fwd Delete

A Closer Look At:
BLOODY MARY

"Bloody Mary is just another vengeful spirit," Eric Kripke notes, "but it's so specific, the game that kids play with each other." As with the telling of most urban legends, there are many versions of the game being played across the country, but most involve a chant in front of the mirror, the most common being simply saying her name in triplicate. However, the more daring add the taunt, "Can't you come out?"

"When you really analyze the game," Kripke continues, "it's ridiculous, because who would want to have this creature appear and claw their eyes out? Why you'd want to play this game is beyond me." Of course, people probably play the game for the same reason they watch *Supernatural* — they do it to scare themselves. They do it for the thrill, the pulse-pounding adrenaline rush.

"I think there's something very troubling and chilling about the idea that you can't see this spirit in reality but it'll appear in the mirror behind you," Kripke confesses. "It's just so classic. People have always been associating ghosts with mirrors. In houses where people recently died, one of the first things that the surviving family used to do was cover all the mirrors, less the reflective surface inadvertently trap that person's soul. There's something about mirrors, about stealing people's souls that is very hardwired in the primal group consciousness of humanity... So I think because of that Bloody Mary is intangibly chilling to us in ways we can't even understand."

SAM: That Bloody Mary legend... Dad ever find any evidence that it was a real thing?
DEAN: Not that I know of.
SAM: I mean, everywhere else, all over the country, kids play Bloody Mary and as far as we know, nobody *dies* from it.
DEAN: Yeah, well, maybe everywhere it's just a story, but here it's actually happening.

"We invented that back-story for her," Kripke says proudly. "What would turn somebody into Bloody Mary? Why would a character show up, and why would it claw your eyes out? Obviously there's not much of an episode if all you have to do is summon it and that's what kills you. And if that's all there is to it, why aren't millions of people across the country dying? So the conceit we came up with is that only if you have a secret will she really appear and kill you."

A Closer Look At:
SHAPESHIFTERS

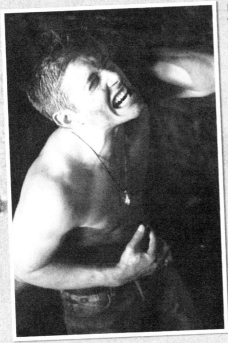

It doesn't matter whether you call it shapeshifting, transmogrification, skinwalking, or anything else, the fact is that it's the ability to change form, from man to animal, animal to man, or man to man. It's an ability that many would kill to have, and even more would kill to destroy — particularly if the shapeshifter in question happens to be attempting to don their skin and bed their beloved...

Every culture in the world has shapeshifter lore. It usually involves animals indigenous to the region, and it often bears similarities to werewolf lore, and occasionally vampire lore. The shapeshifters rarely come by their powers naturally; they tend to either commune with animals' spirits, or fall victim to supernatural bites or curses.

REBECCA: Okay, so this *thing*, it can make itself look like anybody?
SHAPESHIFTER-DEAN: That's right.
REBECCA: Well, what is it? Like a genetic freak?
SHAPESHIFTER-DEAN: Heh. Maybe... Evolution is about mutation, right? So maybe this thing was born human... but was different. *Hideous* and *hated*... until he learned to become someone else.

"How do you find an original way to do a morph?" is the question John Shiban posed to the *Supernatural* team when he was trying to break the story for 'Skin'. "Everyone's done them," he laments. "I have to give credit to Eric for saying, 'Everybody does CGI. Let's not... Is there a way it can be closer to *An American Werewolf in London*?'

"The werewolf transformation is done with prosthetics and makeup. The trick is to do that on a TV budget. But the idea that he's got to shed his skin was what was cool about it. It led to more very cool and helpful story points because if he's shedding his skin, then he's gotta have a place to hide. So that led to the idea of the lair and the sewer, which led to a lot of great set pieces."

It's actually easy to sympathize with the shapeshifter in 'Skin' because he just wants to fit in; he just wants someone to love him. But if you let your guard down, it could be *your* skin the shapeshifter tries to get under. Or worse, a shapeshifter could take on the form of your spouse, your boss, your mother, *anyone*. As Shiban used to say on his previous show, *The X-Files*: "Trust No One."

HOOK MAN

Written by:
John Shiban

Directed by:
David Jackson

Guest Cast: Brian Skala (Rich), Chelah Horsdal (Librarian), Jane McGregor (Lori Sorenson), Alfred E. Humphreys (Sheriff), Christie Laing (Taylor), Mike Waterman (Red Head), Benjamin Rogers (Murph Humphreyville), Dan Butler (Reverend Sorenson), Sean Millington

When Lori Sorenson's boyfriend is murdered in a manner that bears the unmistakable signs of the infamous "Hook Man", Sam and Dean visit a small college town in eastern Iowa. While Dean tries to get on the good side of the girl's reverend father, Sam bonds with her, because having seen Jess murdered, he has an affinity with what she's going through. But Lori's pain and fears are taken to new extremes when her roommate is murdered while she is sleeping. With the police outside, the brothers sneak into Lori's bedroom at her sorority house in order to look for clues. They find a bloody message on her wall straight out of legend: "Aren't you glad you didn't turn on the light?"

Convinced that they are definitely facing the Hook Man, Sam and Dean intensify their research and discover that they're dealing with a vengeful spirit... whose bones are buried in an unmarked grave. Sam keeps an eye on Lori while Dean searches for the grave, but even as Dean is salting and burning the ghost's bones, the Hook Man is terrorizing Sam and the Sorensons.

They realize that since the psycho-killer's murder weapon was actually his replacement hand, it's a part of him and therefore needs to destroyed, too. Further research reveals that the hook was made of silver and re-forged into an unknown object owned by the church. The brothers race to the church, where they battle the dangerous spirit until Sam yanks Lori's silver cross off her neck and Dean burns it.

DEAN: So, you believe her?
SAM: I do.
DEAN: Yeah, I think she's hot, too.

DID YOU KNOW?

Trey Callaway, who wrote the 'Hell House' episode of *Supernatural*, co-wrote *I Still Know What You Did Last Summer*, a movie that features a hook-handed killer.

'Hook Man' was the first episode that co-executive producer John Shiban wrote. "I thought 'Hook Man' was a nice balance of guest character story and brother story. I was pretty pleased with that, and I thought it came out nicely." Thing is, this episode was supposed to air right after 'Wendigo'. "'Wendigo' started with a legend that was fairly well known, but obscure," Shiban observes. "The fun thing about 'Hook Man' was we said from the get-go, 'Let's hit one of the classics, let's go right for the Hook Man.

"It went into production," Shiban continues, "but there were issues with the director. Directing to scare, especially on television, is not as easy as it sounds, and I think that's why so many shows that have tried to be scary have failed. You have to be very specific with point of view, you have to know whose head you're in a scene if you want to build suspense. You have to get only what you need to get and not any

Above

Sam feels a
connection with Lori
Sorenson.

more, because the audience has to be held by the hand to be scared. Unfortunately, we had a director who, I think, got some very good performances, but I don't think he had as much experience in that area as we needed. We ended up moving it back in the schedule, which was frustrating, and re-shooting some pieces of it to try to make it scarier, to try to fulfill the script."

But all was not lost. "There's always happy accidents in life," Shiban remarks. "'Dead in the Water' was directed by Kim Manners, who is phenomenal. It did make a nice stepping stone from 'Wendigo' and onward. Ultimately, 'Hook Man', by the time the re-shoots were done and some re-editing was done, I'm pretty proud of... although I still feel like there was potential in the script that we never got to."

Another happy accident, or as creator Eric Kripke calls it, a "eureka moment", occurred when writers Ron Milbauer and Terri Hughes Burton said, "You know, shotguns shoot salt." To Kripke, "That was the perfect combination of occult element — salt is a folkloric repellant of evil — and the blue-collar aspect of shotguns. The rule

Above

Dean salts and burns the Hook Man's bones.

Opposite

The Hook Man is watching…

I've given the writing staff is, not only do the monsters have to live in real folklore, but the rituals used and methods employed and every aspect of the show has to exist somewhere out there in folklore. You can't just make up a way to kill a monster, you have to find a basis. That was important to me to maintain the credibility of the world."

Good visual effects are also important to the credibility of a supernatural world. Visual effects supervisor Ivan Hayden concurs, and says this episode was "a great challenge. But I think 'Hook Man' was one of my favorite ones to create because it's the first time that I got to turn a guy to ash without any fire. The scare factor of the hook was a simple effect where Randy [Shymkiw, special effects supervisor] created it as a wire behind some plaster, and they pulled the wire, and we removed the wire [in post-production]. But I think a couple of those sort of 'easy' gags, along with the ending shot, really brought the Hook Man alive."

The Hook Man's titular weapon wasn't only created in CG, informs property master Chris Cooper. "The first really cool thing that we made was for the Hook Man — his hook. Designing and building that from scratch, and fitting that on him and making it work was a fun, interesting challenge."

And that hook sure made a racket. "There'll be a lot of times where we'll notice what's a 'sound moment'," explains composer Christopher Lennertz. "One of the things I'd do in 'Hook Man' was that I would play big, big music and there'd be chasing and then he'd run around the corner and disappear and I'd actually take the music out and go all silent so all you heard was *scrrreeeeech* as the thing came and the plaster was coming off their wall — there'd be no music. The music doesn't come in until after he appears. So it actually made it scarier to not have music. Sometimes having big moments of silence makes the music that is there stand out more. We try not to score a scene that doesn't need music."

DEAN: I told him you were a dumbass pledge and that we were hazing you.
SAM: What about the shotgun?
DEAN: I said that you were hunting ghosts and spirits were repelled by rock salt. You know, typical Hell Week prank.
SAM: And he believed you?
DEAN: Well, you look like a dumbass pledge.

Music editor Dino Moriano agrees, pointing out that "that one was creepy". He appreciated how "the music built suspense". And he particularly enjoyed how the combination of music, silence, and scraping caused music supervisor Alexandra Patsavas to sometimes "jump in her seat".

MUSIC

'Merry Go Round'
by Split Habit
'Bang Your Head
(Metal Health)'
by Quiet Riot
'Noise'
by Low Five
'At Rest'
by APM
'Royal Bethlehem'
by APM
'U Do 2 me
(Original Mix)'
by Paul Richards
'Peace of Mind'
by Boston

BUGS

Written by: Rachel Nave, Bill Coakley

Directed by: Kim Manners

Guest Cast: Anne Marie Deluise (Joanie Pike), Jimmy Herman (Jo White Tree), Ryan Robbins (Travis Weaver), Mi-Jung Lee (Newscaster), Jim Byrnes (Professor Reardon), Carrie Genzel (Lynda Bloome), Andrew Airlie (Larry Pike), Tyler Johnston (Matt Pike), Michael Dangerfield (Dustin Burwash)

A construction worker in Oasis Plains, Oklahoma, falls down a sinkhole and dies within minutes when his brain seemingly *dissolves*... Ruling out 'Mad Cow Disease', the Winchester brothers' interest is piqued. They use the open house barbecue thrown by the realtors of the new housing development to snoop around and ask detailed questions about the area. The realtor's son, Matt, who is fascinated with bugs, becomes the prime suspect when it comes to light that another insect-related death occurred in the recent past. That night, while Sam and Dean squat in one of the new homes, a female realtor living a few doors down dies in her shower. The brothers sneak into her house and discover that spiders were behind her death.

When Matt shows them some odd insect behavior in the nearby woods, they discover buried human bones swarming with worms. An investigation into the town's history reveals that the housing development is being built upon ancient Native American land. The local tribe's ancestors cursed it after they'd been forced off by raping and pillaging cavalrymen. The curse proclaims that no white man living on the land will survive the sixth night of the spring equinox, which is that very night.

Sam and Dean hurry back to Matt's house, but his father refuses to leave based on their unbelievable story. Suddenly a massive swarm of bees descends on the house, and they have no choice but to try to wait out the night inside. But bugs come down the chimney and out of every nook and cranny. The brothers and Matt's family keep retreating until they're trapped in the attic with termites opening holes in the ceiling for bees to swarm through. But just when they've lost all hope, the sun rises and the bugs depart.

SAM: Well, dad never treated you like that, you were perfect. He was all over my case. You don't remember?
DEAN: Well, maybe he had to raise his voice, but sometimes you were out of line.
SAM: Right! Right, like when I said I'd rather play soccer than learn bow hunting.
DEAN: Bow hunting's an important skill!

"We just didn't have the time to get those bugs right," Eric Kripke admits. "Bob begged me — everyone begged me — from the beginning not to do it ['Bugs'] because we wouldn't be able to accomplish it on the time and money, and I demanded we go ahead with it anyway. And the result was we weren't able to do what we wanted."

DID YOU KNOW?

All the actors who worked around bees on this episode were given costumes with cuffs sewed on the inside of their pants and sleeves. It helped... but everyone still got stung!

The result didn't surprise director Kim Manners, who'd been one of the people begging Kripke not to do this episode. "Bugs are creepy, but bugs aren't scary," Manners comments.

"It's a really, really hard show to make," Kripke explains, "and you have to pick your battles. We always say to the directors to pick three or four scenes that are really important and spend time on those scenes, and just get the other ones done and move on. We've gotten a lot better about helping in terms of how we conceive ideas in the first place. If you look at the second half of the season, many of our monsters were in human form. Any creature we create has the burden of having to be realistic — you have to do it right or you can't do it."

Working on this episode, and being trapped in a small sealed space with "sixty-thousand stinging bees" was a scary experience for Jensen Ackles. "The guys were releasing the bees on the floor and they just started rising, and this hum, this buzz started filling the air, and they were crawling on you..." Ackles recalls. "I know what I do when I see *one* bee flying around, you know..." He pantomimes running around, waving his hands madly, like most people would do. "They're walking on my face and

I'm just sitting there... And then, of course, when we finally see it, it's all CG bees because they didn't show up on camera. I was so angry! The guy had a stinger in my ass and now they're CG'ing 'em!"

Jared Padalecki also has bad memories of those days on set. "They vacuumed them and then re-released them. The day of shooting, the guy was like, 'You know the more I vacuum them, the more agitated they get, the more they are likely to sting...' And I was like, 'What? You could've been saying this two days ago in rehearsal!'"

Ackles picks up the story. "The great thing was all the crew was in full bee gear, and they're like, 'All right guys, walk on in.' And they've got masks! Gloves! Kim Manners was directing the episode and he walked in in t-shirt and shorts, and popped down on an apple box and said, 'If you guys are gonna be in here, I'm gonna be in here with you.' Then it was like, 'Well, now I *can't* complain.' But he's a cowboy..."

Kripke was also disappointed with the need for CG bees. "They bring in six hundred bees, or however many bees, and I was like, 'Oh my god, I can't wait to see the dailies! But you watch the dailies and you can't tell there's one bee in that room — they just don't read on camera or they were too sluggish. Phil Sgriccia and I were watching the footage and we were like, 'Wait, is that a bee? Is that a bee there?' Sometimes our job is just so absurd. And you just start laughing because you put

mUSIC

'Rock of Ages'
by Def Leppard
'No One Like You'
by Scorpions
'I Got More Bills Than
I Got Pay'
by Black Toast Music
'Poke In Tha Butt'
by Extreme Music
'Medusa'
by MasterSource

your crew in a room with hundreds of bees and then you can't even tell if there are any bees on camera. It's a bizarre job sometimes."

DEAN: Looks like there's only room for one. You want to flip a coin?
SAM: Dean, we have no idea what's down there.
DEAN: All right. I'll go if you're scared. Scared?
SAM: Flip the damn coin!
DEAN: Call it in the air, chicken.

Bees weren't the only insects in 'Bugs'. "We covered a guy with twenty-five thousand beetles," Kim Manners shares. "The beetles kept slipping off that poor guy. Not to mention the fact that he was scared to death. I had a woman lying buck-naked on the floor that I'd put two hundred baby tarantulas on her head, she never whimpered. I had a six-foot-three guy with twelve thousand beetles on him and he cried like a little girl. But the long and short of it is the show wasn't scary."

Opposite
Dean and Sam drive into a "normal" neighborhood.
Below
The brothers give bug-loving Matt Pike a chance to prove his innocence.

A Closer Look At:
THE HOOK MAN

This is a very straightforward legend: a teenage boy takes his virginal girlfriend to "Lover's Lane" to fool around. While there, a radio announcer reports that a murderer, who has a hook in place of his right hand, has escaped from a nearby insane asylum. The couple hear scraping noises outside, but the boy says it's nothing and tries to keep fooling around. The girl resists, and eventually the boy drives her home, where she finds a bloody, detached hook on her door handle.

The legend has expanded over time to include a boyfriend who is too sex-obsessed to take his girlfriend home. He'd rather go outside and look around a bit to allay the girl's fears. The girl hears scratching sounds on the roof of the car and, though terrified, steps outside to call for her boyfriend. She finds him hanging upside down from a tree above the car, his dangling hands brushing against the roof. An offshoot has the girl getting behind the wheel and racing home... where she finds her dead boyfriend pinned to the roof with a bloody hook.

The Hook Man has also been known to sneak into dorm rooms, killing a sexually active teen while her tolerant virgin roommate sleeps in the darkened room. When the girl wakes up, she is horrified to discover that her roommate has been viciously slaughtered, and a message left in blood: "Aren't you glad you didn't turn on the lights?"

DEAN: The hook?
SAM: It was the murder weapon... and in a way it was part of him...
DEAN: So, like the bones, the hook is the source of his power.
SAM: So, if we find the hook, we stop the Hook Man...

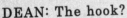

"We kind of borrowed from three or four Hook Man-*ish* urban legends to make it our own," John Shiban acknowledges. "There are two twists: he's the *ghost* of a guy with a hook — not a guy with a hook from an insane asylum that just escaped — and he's attached himself to the conflicting emotions of this girl, almost like a poltergeist would. But the types of scares are exactly what you would expect in a Hook Man story. You're gonna see the guy with the hook trying to kill you."

From the very beginning, the Hook Man urban legend has been a parental warning against premarital sex and promiscuity. In other words, you teenage couples shouldn't be out there parked in lover's lane or alone in dark college dorm rooms, because this psycho killer's gonna get you...

A Closer Look At:

CREEPY CRAWLERS

"There really are a lot of great urban legends about bugs," Eric Kripke emphasizes. "There are tapeworms climbing out of people's mouths, and there are spiders laying eggs in people's brains after which all these spiders pour out."

Earwigs got their name because they like to crawl into people's ears and eat their brains. Love Bugs got their name because they were created in a lab to mate with (and sterilize) mosquitoes, and these overly amorous insects escaped and are so blinded by their lovemaking that they

constantly smash into high-speed motorists, causing countless deadly crashes. And did you know that rabies-infected praying mantis bites can cause women to become cannibalistic during lovemaking? The list goes on and on and on. Name a type of insect and chances are there's an urban legend, or two, about it.

SAM: The question is, why bugs... and why now?
DEAN: That's two questions.

"Let's make an episode about all these urban legends about bugs," Kripke proposed at the start of the process of developing 'Bugs'. "The first draft was great and it was creepy," he recalls. "You send it up to production and they say, 'We can't do it.'" Uh, oh.

"There's no shower legend about bugs! All the bug attacks that ended up in the show weren't the real urban legends of what the bug attacks were. They sorta were 'This is the best we can do with our time and money.' There were lots of rewrites to get things down to budget. It failed. It was a valiant effort..."

The bugs themselves weren't the only story element that failed to live up to Kripke's expectations. "It is a very true and classic urban legend that burial grounds have been desecrated, so therefore certain ancient tribal spirits return for revenge. 'Bugs' was the one time we crossed the line from classic to cliché. Up to that point we'd had very well-known urban legends, but they felt classic and mythic and universal. That was the only time I felt myself rolling my eyes. It felt stale, not fresh. I think we've been very successful at putting fresh spins on classic stories. Once you go to the Indians and the Indian score starts playing on the soundtrack, you can hear the groans nationwide — at least I could — and they haunted my nightmares for days."

So Eric Kripke doesn't have nightmares about monsters, he has nightmares about 'Bugs'...

HOME

Written by: Eric Kripke

Directed by: Ken Girotti

Guest Cast: Jerry Rector (Plumber), Don Thompson (Mike Guenther), Jamie Schwanebeck (Richie Cooper), Haili Page Philippe (Sari Cooper), Kristin Richardson (Jenny Cooper), Loretta Devine (Missouri Mosley)

After Sam has several haunting dreams, he tries to convince Dean to return to their childhood home for the first time since their mother died. When Dean insists on knowing why, Sam admits that his nightmares have been coming true lately, including one about Jessica's death. Dean doesn't know what to make of his brother's newfound supernatural abilities and he has zero desire to return home, but Sam's insistence that people are in danger eventually persuades him.

Back in Lawrence, they are both disappointed and relieved to discover that the malevolent entity terrorizing the house's current occupants — a single mother with two young children — is not the same monster that killed their mother. Based on information in their father's journal, the brothers go to see a local psychic, Missouri Mosley, who joins them in their attempt to rid the house of the increasingly dangerous poltergeist.

Just when they think they've succeeded, the poltergeist comes roaring back and attacks Sam. Then another ghost glides towards them. Dean is ready to blast it with rock salt — when Sam recognizes their mother. In shock, the boys just stare as she approaches them, apologizes to Sam, then turns and "evicts" the unwelcome spirit, sacrificing herself to protect her sons.

> **DEAN:** All right. I've been cruisin' some websites — think I found a few candidates for our next gig. A fishing trawler found off the coast of Cali, its crew vanished. And, uh, we got some cattle mutilations in west Texas. Hey! Am I boring you with this "hunting evil" stuff?
> **SAM:** No, I'm listening. Keep going.
> **DEAN:** And here, a Sacramento man shot himself in the head. Three times. Any of these things blowin' up your skirt, pal?

DID YOU KNOW?

When Sam is getting the children away from the evil spirit, he tells the little girl the same thing his father said to Dean in 'The Pilot': "Take your brother outside as fast as you can. Don't look back."

"We let it just be mythology and emotion," Eric Kripke explains, in discussing their approach to this memorable episode. "We saw how that turned out and we really started to realize that might be the more interesting direction to go in, so we started going into it more and more."

"For 'Home' there actually was a fire-walker," Samantha Smith reveals. "We had a person in a fire suit lit on fire doing the walking. There were scenes we were shooting where I was there alone, where I came down from being 'in fire', with hair blowing and the wind and all that. That was done on a black background to superimpose, sort of like green screen."

"Fire stunts are in and of themselves very dangerous," stunt coordinator Lou Bollo concedes. "If the stunt person for some reason panics in there, and does what a lot of people do and brings in a panicked breath... well, all you're bringing in is a ball of flame and you burn your lungs, and you can essentially consider yourself in very deep trouble at that point. In that particular scene we just needed a shape that could be used for Mary or whoever it was coming out of there. So we used a stunt guy who was smaller and a little bit slimmer than most normal stunt guys, and set him on fire. He had to go on a very specific route. And, of course, you're essentially blind when that's going on. We just rigged up wires that he could feel. And we always have a signal system set up so that whenever the stunt person is starting to feel hot or is burning they drop to the ground and we run and put them out, so that's our safety mechanism."

Above

Missouri Mosley listens to John Winchester's justification for staying away from his sons.

Above

John is aching inside to see his sons.

Another safety mechanism is fireproofing the costumes. "The hardest part when they're wearing nighties and things like that is under-dressing them and making them look like they don't have anything else on," costume designer Diane Widas notes. "In that case, we had a nude Nomax fire-suit. In this instance, Mary's nightie was established in 'The Pilot'. Her nightie was synthetic, which typically you don't use in a burn — it would always be one-hundred percent natural fibers and then you could fireproof it (they still burn, but they burn slower)."

Arguably, though, fiery apparitions were not the scariest things in this episode. "There were some scenes in 'Home' that fed right into fears that you have every day," says executive producer Robert Singer. "There was a guy who fixed the plumbing and stuck his hand down into the sinkerator. Everybody knows what's coming and yells, 'Fast, get it out of there!'"

But he *didn't* get it out of there, not that true horror fans would have it any different. "My favorite scene all year long is the guy grinding up his hand in the garbage disposal," Kripke relates. "We had the shot of underneath the pipe, where you saw the goo going into the bucket, and I laughed because I'm a sick puppy. Everyone around here knows they've come up with something really scary if I start laughing gleefully." The expectation was that the network wouldn't let them keep that take in, but Kripke wanted to use the cut and hope for the best. "I just thought that was the wildest thing to see. And no one said anything. We kept looking at each other, me and Bob and the editors. I can't believe we got that on the air. 'Nightmare' was the only episode where they spoke out and said it was too graphic. I just love that we get away with what we do."

DEAN: Just slow down, would ya. I mean, first you tell me that you've got 'the Shining', and then you tell me that I've got to go back home, especially when...
SAM: When what?
DEAN: When I swore to myself that I would never go back there.

Special effects supervisor Randy Shymkiw didn't find the gore level too sickening, either. "I think it was just right. For us, it is about getting the right amount of gore to sell the gag, and I think we did that. Our gags are there to help sell the story to the audience. Sometimes we need to be a little on the gorier side to do that."

"We had some electric cello and some woodwinds in that episode," composer Chris Lennertz recalls. "To me, that was sort of the big emotional one. It wasn't just an insinuation of emotion like when Dean was with the boy [in 'Dead in the Water']. The last cue became a very cinematic musical moment. And for me, it was nice to get that."

Below
A fiery ghost haunts the old Winchester home.

ASYLUM

Written by: Richard Hatem

Directed by: Guy Bee

Guest Cast: John Gray (Teen), Karly Warkentin (Wife), Peter Benson (Rookie/Officer Walter Kelly), Tom Pickett (Officer Daniel Gunderson), Nicholas D'Agosto (Gavin), Brooke Nevin (Katherine/Kat), Norman Armour (Dr. Sanford Ellicott), James Purcell (Dr. James Ellicott), Nancy Bell, Nicole Laplaca (Spirit), Richard Dietl, Lief Bridgman, Roy Campsall

After receiving coordinates in a text message from their father, Sam and Dean go to the Roosevelt Asylum in Rockford, Illinois, to check out rumors that it is haunted by murderous ghosts. Sam makes an appointment with Dr. James Ellicott, a psychiatrist who is the son of the doctor who ran the asylum, Dr. Sanford Ellicott. Sam prods him for information but the tables are turned on him, and he has to talk about himself and his relationship with Dean. Dr. Ellicott does reveal that the hardcore patients were in the south wing. They rioted, and some bodies were never recovered... including his father's.

That night, the brothers visit the asylum, where they find plenty of spirits roaming the halls. While Dean is quick to pull the trigger, none of the apparitions attack them. They also encounter a girl, Kat, who has been separated from her boyfriend, Gavin. It turns out that the ghosts merely wish to talk — after Sam and Dean find Gavin, a ghost whispers the number 137 to Kat, and Dean goes off in search of that room. Inside, he finds evidence that Dr. Sanford Ellicott conducted cruel experiments on his patients, who then revolted and killed him. The evil doctor's spirit imitates Dean's voice to lure Sam away, and then it gets into Sam's head, turning him against his brother.

Sam blasts Dean with the rock salt, then tries Dean's real gun, but it's unloaded. Dean retaliates and knocks him unconscious. Dean goes into a hidden chamber and finds Sanford's corpse. The spirit attacks him, but Dean manages to grab a lighter and set the corpse on fire. The specter dissolves to ash.

SAM: It doesn't matter what he wants —
DEAN: See that attitude right there? That's why I always got the extra cookie.

"'Asylum' was a lot of fun," asserts visual effects supervisor Ivan Hayden. "We did one shot that we all really enjoyed: the gun comes down on the side of a little old lady's head and they pull the trigger and vaporize her into ectoplasmic goo. And we're all just giggling around the computer monitor: 'We're shooting a little old lady in the head!' What other job can you do such twisted stuff? It was pretty funny."

Special effects supervisor Randy Shymkiw cites the scene near the end of this episode, when Dr. Ellicott turns to dust and collapses, as one of the most challenging gags they did. "We had to cast the entire torso as a solid, but when it hit the ground,

DID YOU KNOW?

Riverview Hospital, the large mental health facility used as the titular asylum, has also substituted for a prison, a regular hospital, and an apartment building on different episodes of *Supernatural*.

Above

Dr. Sanford Ellicott
asks Sam for a piece
of his mind.

it had to collapse into dust. Another shot in the effect was Ellicott holding up his hands while we watched them turn to dust and collapse. Finding the right mixture that would keep its form and collapse on impact was a tough one, as we also needed a way for the hands to independently collapse on cue."

"With that episode, it was more about the way we shot it," says key makeup artist Shannon Coppin, "because we had makeup that was really extreme, which isn't really the direction the show wanted to go. They want them to be spooky, so they shot them in a way that you didn't see the whole makeup, but you got the impression of something... What your eye catches and what your brain thinks it saw is the whole point."

As with the subtly-seen makeup, the episode "didn't really hit you over the head with music, it was creepy-crawly in that regard," composer Chris Lennertz says. "It was like a snake sneaking along the ground. Those kind are fun to do because you have to figure out musically where you belong — you have to be part of the ambience. The lighting and the way these shows are shot is also a huge part of what inspires me, certainly — it's not just the storyline or how an actor is getting through a scene. If something is shot a certain way, it speaks volumes about what colors to use musically and what tone and what dynamic level."

Key hairstylist Jeannie Chow ruminates on the spirits that haunt Riverview, the

Above

Sam works out some issues he has with his brother.

mUSIC

'Hey You'
by Bachman-Turner Overdrive

old asylum where this episode was filmed. "Because we film there so much — there are two floors that we film in all the time — I think it's been self-cleansed. There's not a lot of activity there. But you go where there's not as much filming going on, and I think that's where all the spirits have gone to. You just don't want to be caught in the basement by yourself. Sometimes I'll be wandering down the hall by myself — it's a big building — and I'll walk in the wrong direction because it's a bit of a maze. The building is built in a labyrinth, where you have to walk through another room to continue down a hallway, then a hallway sort of does a u-turn and puts you in a different direction... I think they built it that way to confuse the patients. It still gives you a creepy vibe."

Set decorator George Neuman agrees. "As many times as I've been down there, it's still creepy. I really don't like hospitals — that clinical sort of lighting and the smell, it's still there, even though the walls have been painted a thousand times by different film crews. It still creeps me out."

But, of course, they did do a lot to it to give it the textured look seen in the episode. "It was a phenomenal breakdown," costume designer Diane Widas enthuses. "We

DEAN: Hey, I got a question for ya. You seen a lot of horror movies, yeah?
KAT: I guess so.
DEAN: Do me a favor, next time you see one... pay attention. When someone says a place is haunted, don't go in.

used a lot of puff paint and different things that are kind of unusual breakdown techniques. And wax. And to get some of the cobwebbing and stuff, we used glue guns and things like that. We just had a lot of fun making it look gross."

However, it was two other elements that made the episode stand out for John Shiban. "'Asylum' is interesting in that that's the first time we established iron as a spirit deterrent," he remarks. And the character Kat "came from a desire not to play to the cliché. And so from the very beginning it's like, 'Let's not make her the one who's screaming, useless and helpless, let's make it the guy.' And I just love that. It's just nice to turn it on its head. I've always had strong women in my life and I've always liked characters like that. And Brooke Nevin really nailed it. We enjoyed her. She was cool."

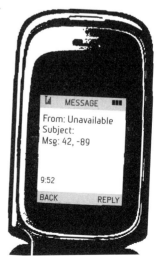

SCARECROW

Written by: John Shiban
Directed by: Kim Manners

Guest Cast: Lara Gilchrist (Holly), Brendan Penny (Steve), William B. Davis (Professor), Tania Saulnier (Emily), Tom Butler (Harley Jorgeson), P. Lynn Johnson (Stacey Jorgeson), Brent Stait (Scotty), Leah Graham (Pauly), Angela Moore (Clerk), Christian Schrapff (Vince), Tim O'Halloran (Scotty), David Orth (Sheriff), Mike Carpenter (The Scarecrow)

Sam and Dean finally make contact with their father, but he tells them to stop looking for him because it's not safe. Instead, he sends them on a new mission. Frustrated with their father's evasiveness, Sam decides to search for him, but Dean refuses. They go their separate ways, with Dean driving the Impala to Burkitsville, a small town in Indiana where couples have gone missing on the same day each year for at least three years.

Everyone in Burkitsville appears uneasy with Dean's questions except for a girl named Emily, who remembers seeing the most recently disappeared couple. Emily also tells him that the town seems to be blessed. Dean's suspicions are aroused when the townsfolk seem to want to get rid of him, while they're busy "fattening up" a young couple whose car just happened to break down at the local gas station. Meanwhile, Sam meets an intriguing young drifter, Meg, and when she talks about her dysfunctional family, they find they have a lot in common. Dean is run out of town by the sheriff, but he returns after dark in time to save the young couple from an animate scarecrow.

Dean checks in with Sam and they conclude that the scarecrow is a manifestation of a pagan god that takes the couples as fertility sacrifices. They grunt apologies and swap compliments, but remain separated. Dean meets with a local professor and learns the pagan god draws its energy from a sacred tree. But shortly after, he's abducted by the sheriff, who throws him into a cell with Emily. When Sam can't reach Dean, he changes direction and heads to Burkitsville, despite Meg's arguments. Sam frees Dean and Emily, but the scarecrow has vanished from its perch. The locals surround them, but it turns out the pagan god isn't particular about its sacrificecs and takes Emily's aunt and uncle instead. The next morning the brothers find the sacred tree and give Emily the pleasure of torching it. Sam tells Dean he's sticking with him. Meanwhile, we learn that Meg is some sort of demonic spy.

DID YOU KNOW?

The apple trees in 'Scarecrow' were actually hazelnut trees.

SAM: So, dad is sending us to Indiana to go hunting for something before another couple vanishes?
DEAN: Yahtzee. Can you imagine putting together a pattern like this? The different obits dad had to go through? The man's a master!

"The scarecrow sent chills up my spine," admits Robert Singer. "That one got to me. I think a lot of it was the way Kim shot it, being out in this orchard at night. The

whole thing was really spooky. For the scare level, I like that one a lot."

"One of my favorite moments of the season was in that show," Jensen Ackles reveals. "When the young couple in the teaser are walking by the scarecrow... and you just see his head move and catch the girl's eye. I didn't expect that — that wasn't in the script. I remember when I saw that, I was like, 'Whoa, freaky!'" His onscreen brother also liked this episode. "'Scarecrow' was really good," Jared Padalecki says. "And in my opinion one of the scarier ones."

"I designed and we built the entire costume," recalls costume designer Diane Widas of the episode's titular character. "He had to wear a harness underneath his costume and we had to allow for that in order for them to hang him there, so that it was safe for him. Mike Carpenter was a really good sport because this was probably a really hard costume for him to wear. From a costuming standpoint though, the scarecrow was fabulous."

"The special effects makeup team made a mask and I made a wig and we put it

Above

Emily, Sam, and Dean encounter a mob of angry townsfolk.

all together with the wardrobe," adds key hairstylist Jeannie Chow. "He was really creepy. And he was a trooper because the material they used to make the mask is made out of that foam latex which smells like rotten eggs."

DEAN: What made you change your mind?
SAM: I didn't. I still want to find dad... and you're still a pain in the ass. But Jess and mom — they're both gone. Dad is god knows where. You and me, we're all that's left. So, uh, if we're gonna see this through, we're gonna do it together.
DEAN: Hold me, Sam. That was beautiful.

MUSIC

'Bad Company'
by Bad Company
'Lodi'
by Creedence
Clearwater Revival
'Puppet'
by Colepitz

"We brought in a great character named Meg, played by Nicki Aycox," executive producer Kim Manners points out. "We started a mythology that the show desperately needed." Production designer Jerry Wanek concurs: "When Nicki came to our show, I thought that was a great foil for our boys. She's a fine actress." Talking about Nicki, Padalecki says, "She was great. No matter how tough the dialogue, or how demanding the scripts were of her, she really did an excellent performance across the board and made the episodes that much better."

There was one scene in 'Scarecrow' that proved particularly challenging for Nicki

Aycox. "It doesn't seem that real to me," recalls the actress of the scene in which she slits a man's throat. "I have to say that sometimes I do think about whether or not I feel bad that maybe children watch it and what they might think. Sometimes that does bother me a little bit, but I try to move forward."

"That was an episode I really liked a lot," editor David Ekstrom comments. "I thought Meg was a neat character. I liked that storyline happening at the same time — keeping the audience guessing as to whether this was a potential romantic situation with Jared — what was going on with that.

"I think another reason I really like 'Scarecrow' is that the scarecrow was really creepy-looking," Ekstrom continues. "And part of what was really creepy about it was it was just there in daylight. It's broad daylight, Dean goes up on a ladder and is looking into the face of the scarecrow. And I would venture to say everyone who was watching that show was creeped out entirely by how close his face got to that thing; and you were ready for 'Boo!' at any second. Anticipation is a big factor; you can terrify a person with anticipation. Dean's face next to that scarecrow — nothing happened. But when I think of that episode, that scene comes to mind as being one of the scary scenes — *nothing happened*! It was all anticipation: 'Don't get near that thing! His eyes are gonna open!'"

Below
Sam and Dean discover that the scarecrow has vanished.

A Closer Look At:
VENGEFUL SPIRITS

What happens when we die? Practically every culture throughout the world, throughout history, has believed that our soul — our *spirit* — lives on in some form. Ideally, we move on to a heavenly plain of existence, but what happens when we don't move on?

"That's kind of spooky," key makeup artist Shannon Coppin exclaims, "because it makes you wonder, are you going to know when you're dead? Are we even having this conversation?"

Legends stretching back over the ages speak of ghosts haunting buildings, boats, waterways, roadways, and more recently, automobiles, airplanes, and even space stations. Question is, why are these spirits hanging around? Coppin believes she knows. "They're people that died a certain way [such as murder, suicide, or unexpected heart attacks] and they never got peace and eventually they kind of go crazy, and they become more and more disgruntled throughout the years being caught in limbo..." Often these disgruntled ghosts have childlike tantrums where they throw objects around, shake beds, and slam doors. But the poltergeists that are truly angry are known to get violent — they throw knifes, knock plugged-in hairdryers into bathtubs, and push people down stairs.

DEAN: The only thing that makes me more nervous than a pissed-off spirit... is the pissed-off spirit of a psycho-killer.

An example of a vengeful spirit is Doctor Ellicott in 'Asylum', which Eric Kripke cites as one of his favorite ghost-story episodes. "It's the evocative setting that makes it unique." On the other hand, 'Route 666' was his least favorite ghost episode. But with the show often described as "*Star Wars* and Route 66", and the 'number of the beast' being 666, a Route 666 episode was inevitable. "There really was a Route 666 in the American west," Kripke notes. "And there was talk of a phantom truck that would terrorize drivers."

"The cool thing about Sam and Dean chasing down these spirits is once they catch them, they end the pain that they're in by releasing them," Coppin reflects. "Because often this isn't a bad person, this is someone who was caught in a set of circumstances and they were just somebody's daughter or somebody's wife who was murdered maliciously and they just have to find peace." Isn't that what we're all hoping for when we die?

A Closer Look At:

PAGAN SCARECROWS

Pagan gods are the personification of aspects of nature and the universe. Since they are gods, they generally can assume any form they choose, but they tend to take on human or animal aspects. Their worshippers perform rituals in order to gain bountiful harvests, good health, fertility, wealth, and protection from other deities. And in order to secure these blessings, they provide human sacrifices in appeasement.

Norse mythology is probably best known for such gods as Thor, Odin, and Loki, who belong to the subgroup Aesir, but there are also many minor gods that belong to the subgroup Vanir… who are the ones for whom villages built effigies — the forebears of scarecrows — in their fields. When the Vanir wish to communicate with their subjects or devour the sacrificial offerings, they often possess these effigies.

EMILY: I don't understand… They're going to kill us?
DEAN: Sacrifice us. Which is, I don't know, classier I guess.

"The Norse god that we came up with was one of those things where we have to seek out the right folklore to combine with the character that we want to do," explains Eric Kripke. "We knew we wanted to do a scarecrow episode, and there are a lot of great urban legends and stories about scarecrows that come to life and kill people… just really classic American pastoral, gothic stories about these scarecrows. And that's just really creepy and scary. It's very distinctly American — farms and cornfields and scarecrows. (Of course, they don't have cornfields up in Vancouver, so it became an apple orchard, but same difference.) So it was a question of, how do we bring that scarecrow to life? And we had done so many ghosts up to that point that we wanted to do something different."

Diane Widas designed the effigy to look inhuman. "We did a little straw pad for underneath so that he would look like a straw man, and then we pulled out tufts to help sell that it was a straw guy as opposed to a real person. The scarecrow was fabulous — it was so creepy and horrific." John Shiban agrees: "The stuffed man that comes to life, even in *The Wizard of Oz*, is just so creepy."

FAITH

Written by: Raelle Tucker, Sera Gamble

Directed by: Allan Kroeker

Guest Cast: Rebecca Jenkins (Sue Ann Le Grange), Tiffany Lyndall-Knight (Doctor), Conrad Whitaker (Burly Cop #1), Pat Waldron (Elderly Lady), Jim Codrington (Doctor), Alex Diakun (The Reaper), Rikki Gagne (Holly Morton), Kevin McNulty (Roy Le Grange), Shawn Reis (Burly Cop #2), Woody Jeffreys (Marshall Hall), Scott Miller (Cop #1), Aaron Craven (David Wright), Colin Lawrence (Jason), Julie Benz (Layla Roarke), Gillian Barber (Mrs. Roarke), Erica Carroll (Nurse), John Hainsworth, Cainan Wiebe (Boy), Kenya Jo Kennedy, Nick Harrison

While battling a Rawhead, an Irish hobgoblin that preys on naughty children, Dean is electrocuted, causing permanent damage to his heart... and leaving him with less than a month to live! Distraught, Sam searches frantically for a way to save his brother and believes he may have found it when he hears of Roy Le Grange, a faith healer who appears to be the real deal. Blinded by his desire to save Dean, Sam doesn't question the source of the preacher's powers and convinces Dean to give it a shot. Thinking he has nothing to lose, a nonetheless skeptical Dean goes to see Le Grange and is selected for healing. To Sam's relief, Dean is cured. However, Dean feels guilty because a young woman named Layla, who has a brain tumor, has been visiting the preacher for a long time, patiently waiting her turn.

Dean's guilt multiplies exponentially when he discovers that at the exact same moment of every healing, someone else dies. It seems Le Grange is using black magic to bind a Reaper to his will. They debate killing him, but they don't kill human beings. Instead they plan to destroy his spell book. And when they return to church, Dean finds himself in the uncomfortable position of trying to convince Layla not to go through with her healing, now that it's finally her turn. She ignores him, so instead he shouts "Fire!" and clears the congregation. But the Reaper is still stalking its latest victim... and that's when they realize that Le Grange's wife is the one controlling the Reaper. She turns the Reaper on Dean, but Sam manages to find the source of her power, an amulet, and smashes it. Unleashed, the Reaper leaves Dean and turns on its former master.

DEAN: Hey, you better take care of that car, or I swear I'll haunt your ass.
SAM: I don't think that's funny...
DEAN: Aw, come on... it's a little funny.

"My favorite episode is 'Faith'," Eric Kripke notes. "It's when I first realized what the show was capable of. Here's this episode about: Is there a god? What's meant to be? And is there free will? And is your life worth the cost of someone else's life? It's a metaphysical and moral study of the boys' universe. There's so many different places

the show can go and so many tones. That's been really fun to do.

"The impetus of that episode was, Dean dies in the teaser and how do you save Dean's life? What if you can find someone who could save Dean's life, but at the cost of someone else's life? How do you feel about that moral choice? Do you stop that choice from being made when good people are being brought back to life and other people are having their lives taken away? I thought it was sort of interesting because it raised the question that maybe we shouldn't stop this. That's why the character Layla was so valuable. She's really a great girl and she deserves to live, and some stranger you don't even know will die... and maybe that's worth it. That's what the episode's really about and it was only me saying, 'Well, what's the monster?' In the first couple of versions there was no monster, just the faith healer. And I was like, 'Well guys, what are the scare sequences going to look like? How does he have the power to control life and death anyway?' And that's where we came up with: Well, if he's able to control a real grim reaper, you can send the reaper to harvest some souls and then give other souls back. And you can have the scare sequences where the reaper is after you."

"My favorite episode was 'Faith'," Robert Singer notes, echoing Kripke. "That episode, in addition to having an antagonist in the reaper, it said something, it commented on what's going on today. Julie Benz was terrific, and she and Jensen had

some really great moments."

Writer Sera Gamble recalls that they "started with the idea of faith healers as scary creatures. There's lots you can say about people who twist religion for their own good..." Gamble was surprised that the hot-button topics explored in the episode didn't raise any red flags with the producers, studio, or network. "I kept expecting someone to say, 'No, no, no'... but no one did. They put a lot of faith in us."

Gamble's co-writer Raelle Tucker had a similar reaction. "It's so shocking. I am so surprised, I gotta tell you. Sera and I, when we were conceiving of it, were like, 'It's not gonna happen. Let's be realistic.' And this is a mistake that all established writers make: you immediately start to question what you're allowed to do on television before you really even try to do it. So we end up with kind of safe stories a

MUSIC

'Don't Fear the Reaper'
by Blue Oyster Cult

lot of the time across the board on TV because we're scared. We almost censored ourselves, but then we didn't. And everybody seemed really passionate about this idea and wanted to put it on the air and nobody questioned it."

DEAN: It must be rough, to believe in something so much and have it disappoint you like that.
LAYLA: You wanna hear something weird? I'm okay. Really. I guess if you're gonna have faith, you can't just have it when the miracles happen. You have to have it when they don't.

Composer Chris Lennertz reveals, "We recorded on a seventy-six-key smaller piano, which would've made sense because they were traveling evangelists, so they would've used a smaller, more portable, easily carried piano. The piano, which actually was the piano that they used on tour with Jefferson Airplane in the early seventies, was all beat up and sort of out of tune. Allan Silva played the piano on this episode. We went to his house and spent about two or three hours just taping things to the keys, like fishing line, old coins, paper clips... You hear things rattling, so it sounds really creaky and weird, and old and crappy. That came off really cool."

Even cooler, though, was Lennertz's use of "an Armenian duduk. It's a really creepy sort of microtonal snake charmer instrument, which to me made perfect sense because it had a snake-oil salesman vibe. So if you listen carefully, you hear a little bit of that sell-you-a-bill-of-goods vibe mixed in with the scariness of the show." ✄

Opposite

Sam watches in horror as the Reaper takes its revenge on Sue Ann Le Grange.

Below

Hiding from a Rawhead, the children are relieved to see Sam and Dean.

ROUTE 666

Written by:
Eugenie Ross-Leming and Brad Buckner

Directed by:
Paul Shapiro

Guest Cast: Gary Hetherington (Mayor Harold Todd), Alvin Sanders (Jimmy Anderson), Kathleen Noone (Audrey Robinson), Megalyn Echikunwoke (Cassie Robinson), Dee Jay Jackson (Cyrus Dorian), Mike Busswood, Ron Robinson

D ean is contacted by Cassie Robinson, a girl he once dated, who asks him to come to Mississippi to investigate her father Martin's murder, which is part of a string of racially motivated killings that she thinks could have a paranormal connection. Each murder is linked to a mysterious black truck that seems to be driverless and leaves no tracks. Sam is amazed to see a different side of his playboy brother, but annoyed that Dean shared their secret with a girl he hadn't known that long. As Dean struggles to come to grips with the residual feelings he has for Cassie, the town's white mayor is murdered.

That night, the black truck threatens Cassie in her home, but disappears before Sam and Dean arrive. Cassie's mother, Audrey, confesses that years ago, when she left her boyfriend Cyrus Dorian for Martin, a black man, Cyrus had flown into a rage and burned down the church where Audrey and Martin were going to get married. Then Cyrus tried to kill Martin, but Martin turned the tables and beat Cyrus to death. Audrey reveals that the mayor was a deputy back then who'd turned a blind eye to what he saw as justified self-defense.

They pull up Cyrus's truck from the swamp where Martin hid it, and torch the body they find inside, but the black truck comes after them anyway. Dean drives off to lure the truck away and tells Sam to burn the real truck. A chase ensues and Sam directs Dean to park on the spot where the church that Cyrus burned down used to be, and after a nerve-wracking near head-on collision, the ghost truck is vaporized upon crossing the hallowed ground.

SAM: You *told* her? You told her! The *secret*? Our big family rule number one: We do what we do, and we shut up about it! For a year and a half I do nothing but lie to Jessica, and you go out with this chick in Ohio a couple of times and you tell her *everything*? Dean!
DEAN: Yeah, looks like it.

"The ghost truck just wasn't as scary as we'd hoped it'd be," Eric Kripke concedes. "At the end of the day, it just looked like a monster truck. One of the original conceptions was Dean in a drag race with a phantom vehicle. The Impala vs the monster — they have to race to the death! That's my favorite part of the episode, that climax when Dean is driving and the truck is on his tail and screeching around corners. But because we couldn't afford a whole episode of car chases, which is what

I really would've liked, we had to fill it out with a story. We came up with this plot about the racist truck, which looking back is totally ridiculous. It was just one of those stories that didn't work. It got a little on the nose with all that exploration of racial tensions in the sixties."

Special effects supervisor Randy Shymkiw has a different view of this episode: "One of my favorite episodes has to be 'Route 666'. It kept up a high-paced, exciting kind of scary that worked really well.

"For 'Route 666', we had a lot of stunts that were a lot of fun, most notably when the car had to go off the pipe-ramp and flipped. The car was on a cable that went through a pulley that was bull-pricked to the road and then attached to a truck that pulled it, with sparks on the bottom that we had to visually time. We knew we had to get the car going forty miles an hour and have it hit the ramp just right, so it was a fairly intense gag. It took a lot of preparation but it all went well, and I'm really happy with how it turned out."

"For 'Route 666', we were supposed to be on the Bayou, and we had a freak snow storm," key hairstylist Jeannie Chow recalls. "Of course, it doesn't really snow in Louisiana! That was a fun day, though, for Jared and Jensen, because they're both from Texas and they don't get to see a lot of snow. We went tobogganing and had a snowball fight!"

"Because it was snowing and the water tables were so high, it all turned to mud and snow slush and the truck got stuck," key makeup artist Shannon Coppin explains, "but because they're from Texas and they're used to mud and stuff, [Jensen and Jared] got out and they were digging out the truck. It was pretty funny. They'd rather do that than sit in a hot tent. They're all into getting muddy and doing it bad-ass style."

It seems everyone had fun on this shoot. "'Route 666' was a riot to work on," comments location manager Russ Hamilton. "At one point in the episode, you see the truck being pulled out of the pond... Well, what nobody saw was the tractor that was pulling it out... and there were two other tractors pulling that tractor because the mud was so deep nobody could get in there. That was a really fun one. At the end of the night, after eighteen hours — it was like four o'clock in the morning — there were about fifteen of us having a mud fight. And we're all grown adults, we should be so much past that..."

"The drama was not as strong as the coolness of the ghost truck," executive

MUSIC

'Walk Away'
by James Gang
'She Brings Me Love'
by Bad Company
'Can't Find My Way Home'
by Steve Winwood
(re-recorded)

producer John Shiban contends. "What happens on the road is all nice and scary, but I just didn't think that the story held together. There's a lot of pressure, obviously, from networks to have romance. It's tricky on our show. They're so much the guys who come into town, solve the problem, and move on. The minute you start giving them roots beyond the family, I think it starts to stretch the franchise in a way that just doesn't work, that doesn't feel right. They're professionals, they're superheroes, they're on a mission. And the minute they turn away from that mission, it can diminish them as characters if you're not really careful. 'Why aren't you saving people? You're having sex, you're having fun, you're enjoying yourself — you should be stopping the monster!'"

SAM: So, burning the body had no effect on that thing?
DEAN: Sure it did. Now it's *really pissed*.

"The violence we don't get a lot of notes on," editor Anthony Pinker says. But for this episode, "The note I got from the network was, 'The girl can't be on top.' But I had a guy run off the road, and another guy got completely crushed inside 'cause a pickup truck ran him over... But, y'know, can't have a girl on top. I couldn't figure that one out." ✏

Opposite

Sam and Dean burn the corpse of ghost truck driver Cyrus Dorian.

Below

Dean and Sam examine the scene of the mayor's murder.

NIGHTMARE

Written by: Sera Gamble, Raelle Tucker

Directed by: Philip Sgriccia

Guest Cast: Beth Broderick (Alice Miller), Brendan Fletcher (Max Miller), Avery Raskin (Roger Miller), Dalias Blake (Cop), Cameron McDonald (Jim Miller), Susinn McFarlen (Nosy Neighbor), Fred Keating (Kenneth Phillips)

Sam has a premonition in which a man is murdered by invisible forces, but the killing is made to look like a suicide. Sam convinces Dean they must go to Saginaw, Michigan, but they arrive too late to save the man. The next day, they visit the house pretending to be priests and meet the victim's brother, Roger, wife, Alice, and son, Max. The brothers are puzzled when they fail to find any indication of a supernatural presence. That night, Sam gets excruciating head pains along with a vision of Roger getting decapitated in his apartment.

Roger doesn't heed their warnings and dies a gruesome, unexplainable death. Dean suspects the family itself is cursed and they look into the Millers' history. They talk to a neighbor who reveals Joe and Roger both beat Max regularly, while his stepmother did nothing. Sam is overwhelmed by another vision, this time of Max murdering his stepmother with telekinesis. They arrive at the house in time to save Alice, but a suspicious Max seals the house. He confides in Sam that his mother died pinned to the ceiling when he was a baby.

Sam tells him they must be connected in some way. But Max's rage takes over and he shuts Sam into a closet. Then Max apparently shoots Dean in the head! This horrific vision kick-starts Sam's own telekinetic abilities, which he uses to escape the closet. He saves Dean and appeals to Max, who realizes he can't fix things... and shoots himself. Later, Sam asks Dean if he's concerned about the possibility of him losing control like Max, but Dean assures him it'll never happen if they stick together.

SAM: Well, don't look at me like that.
DEAN: I'm not looking at you like anything... But I gotta say, you look like crap.
SAM: Nice. Thanks.

"It's a bigger, epic storyline that we were starting up," explains the episode's director, Phil Sgriccia. An epic storyline heralded by the return of *the* demon. This is the episode composer Christopher Lennertz had been waiting for. "The thing that I'm hoping everyone picked up on is this is when the demon-thing came back," he says, referring to the "clanky, nasty" music motif introduced in 'The Pilot'. "When Sam was sitting there with the kid, we placed it exactly to the realization of Sam. It was such a big moment for me to be able to bring that back finally and go, 'There's the spot.'"

"The show was supposed to take place in Saginaw, Michigan," comments Sgriccia.

"I'm from Michigan. And we used two early Bob Seger songs because he's from Detroit, Michigan. We tend to try to tailor some of the soundtrack to where we're at in the country. The lodge that they stayed at was like a hunting lodge: dead animals, stuffed animals, log cabin type of feel. I actually got my sister who lives in the Upper Peninsula to send me some coffee mugs and baseball caps, all sorts of Michigan stuff. In fact, in one scene when the boys interview a guy, he's wearing a cap that says Elk Rapids — that's where I went to high school."

Another notable costume choice in the episode is when the brothers pose as priests. "They were very cute little priests," costume designer Diane Widas says with a grin. "They're very handsome boys, so they were supposed to look like their clothes didn't quite fit them perfectly. Jensen, his pants are always a little short, too tight. He's supposed to be a little bit more blue-collar than Sam. We've always tried to maintain that in his style."

Of the key scene where Max threatens his stepmother with a knife, Sgriccia states, "We show enough to get you squeamish. Our visual effects guys came up with the teardrop idea. It was just freaky when we saw their first pass at it because they didn't tell us. It really made it real, because up until that point nothing had touched

Above

Dean is concerned by Sam's painful vision.

her, and audiences are savvy enough now that they kinda know it's some form of visual effect, but by puncturing the tear, it made it very, very real and very creepy and eerie."

SAM: We're not gonna kill Max.
DEAN: Then what? Hand him over to the cops and say, "Lock him up, officer, he kills with the power of his mind"?

MUSIC

'2+2=?'
by Bob Seger
'Lucifer'
by Bob Seger

Writer Sera Gamble argues that the show "cannot be exploitive and gory enough" for her. "I'm always looking to top myself with goriness. Common practice in television is to shoot scenes that will get censored so that they can keep other scenes." But editor David Ekstrom agrees with Sgriccia: "I think slowly putting that knife through the eyeball probably would have been a bit much for most audiences — they probably didn't want to see that."

Episode co-writer Raelle Tucker, however, is more interested in the characters than the gore level. "I guess I'm personally obsessed with these characters, with a morality you can't entirely understand, you can't judge one way or another. [Like] the idea that Max was doing these horrible things, but it's somehow very defensible. In a certain way, all the villains that I end up writing are villains that you want to sympathize with on some level... and I don't know what that says. You just kind of want to take him home and take care of him. Which is why we struggled a lot with how to end that episode, and he ends up killing himself. On a certain level these guys' job should be to off Max, but can we watch the boys do that and still be okay with them? Because, if we've done this right, then we're gonna somehow care about this kid. And we also couldn't just let him live because we knew he would continue to do horrible things." ✍

Below
Dean uses his homemade EMF meter to search for supernatural activity.

THE BENDERS

Written by: John Shiban

Directed by: Peter Ellis

Guest Cast: Ken Kirzinger (Jared Bender), Shawn Reis (Lee Bender), John Dennis Johnston (Abraham Bender), Sandra Steier (Barfly), Alexia Fast (Missy Bender), Sadie Lawrence (Mrs. McKay), Jessica Steen (Officer Kathleen Hudak), Ryan Drescher (Evan McKay), Jon Cuthbert (Alvin Jenkins)

A young boy witnesses a man vanish into thin air, so Sam and Dean investigate. They've barely stepped foot in the small town of Hibbing, Minnesota, when Sam vanishes too, leaving Dean scrambling to figure out what supernatural monster abducted his brother. Passing himself off as a police officer, Dean convinces the local deputy, Kathleen, to help him track down the phantom abductors.

Sam awakes in a cage beside the missing man, Jenkins. Two hooded figures bring them food, and Sam is surprised they're not monsters. Kathleen learns that Dean's not really an officer, but sympathizes with him since her brother disappeared the same way. Meanwhile, Sam frees himself and Jenkins, *too* easily, so he hangs back while Jenkins runs. His cell door immediately locks shut again, by remote... and he soon hears Jenkins screaming. Sam's captors hunt other humans for the twisted pleasure of it.

Dean and Kathleen arrive at a backwoods home, and Kathleen handcuffs Dean to her squad car before investigating. Dean uses the car's antenna to get free, then finds Sam — and Kathleen — caged in a barn. He searches the house for a key to the cells, but instead finds the family's "trophies" and photos of them with their victims. He's caught off guard by a teenage girl, who stabs him. Her father and two large brothers appear and tie Dean to a chair. Pa Bender boasts they've been hunting humans for generations, then tells Dean that Sam's next. But Sam and Kathleen get the jump on their captors. While Sam goes to find Dean, Pa Bender laughs about killing Kathleen's brother, so she shoots him. She suspects the bothers have something to hide, so tells them to hit the road before more police arrive.

PA BENDER: Tell me, any other cops gonna come lookin' for you?
DEAN: Oh, eat me! No, no, no... wait, wait. You actually might.

"How do you do *Texas Chain Saw Massacre* in a supernatural setting, and for television?" John Shiban recalls the writers pondering. "It's such a classic situation. A twist would be that it's not supernatural — that would be a surprising twist. Because they're going to be expecting alien cannibals from the future come back to do whatever. For the Winchesters, of all the things they've faced, even being raised by their dad, that's something they haven't encountered. And then it's an opportunity for some very fun reveals and surprises for them. When you think about it, so many

Above

Lee and Missy Bender
want Dean to stay
awhile.

monsters are akin to natural phenomena — it's about survival and existence... but it's not as diabolical and twisted as a human being can get. Some of our nastiest nasties have been partly human, whether it's possessed humans or mutant humans. Only a human being would ever kill anyone just for fun."

"The little girl in 'The Benders' with greasy hair is arguably the scariest character we had this season," executive producer Eric Kripke states.

Jensen Ackles certainly agrees. "She freaked me right out — throwing knifes at me and screaming 'Daddy' and stuff..." he says with a shudder. "There wasn't a whole lot of acting I had to do for that — I was freaked right out." Regarding that scene with Ackles, co-executive producer John Shiban points out, "If she had been even ten percent off, the moment becomes a laugh, not a scare. And that little girl just nailed it. Even from the casting tape, she just had a quality that makes the hair go up on the back of your neck..."

Costume designer Diane Widas recalls a sweeter side to the young actress. "I made her dress and as I recall it was *absolutely* disgusting — she was a really good sport." The rest of the Bender family actors, along with the costumers themselves, didn't have it easy, either. "We had to make it look like they'd lived in their clothes, and it's very arduous to make it look that bad."

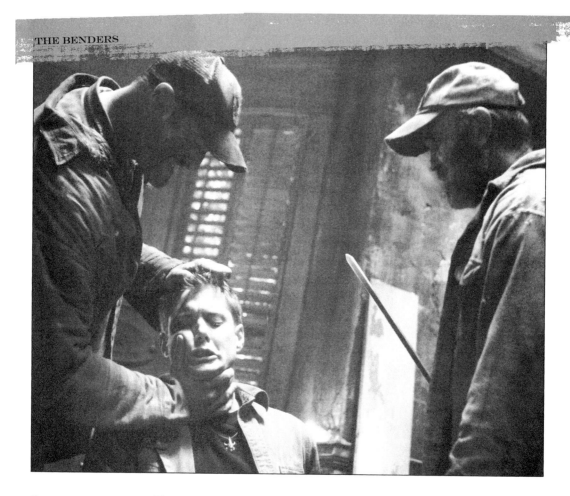

Above

Jared and Pa Bender interrogate Dean.

MUSIC

'Rocky Mountain Way'
by Joe Walsh
'Sweet and Low Down'
by Composer

The actors' clothes weren't the only disgusting things on their bodies. Key makeup artist Shannon Coppin remembers "making them dirty; making their hair greasy and making their skin look dirty. It's one of those things where it's not, 'You fall down and have a piece of dirt on you' — it's this grime that gets into the cracks of your skin. This grime that resonates all over your body, and you can't really tell what it is, you just know these people never bathe. That's got to be a very subtle look, believable right down to their fingernails and under their nails and behind their ears and in their ears and in their teeth. That's what sells the characters, believable details."

Property master Chris Cooper is into the details, too. "A cool thing we did on 'The Benders' was the big spear. We had to make a retractable version and a rubber version. Stuff like that is always fun to create, to figure out how the director cams specific shots and how it's gonna work because you have to hide certain parts of it. We make blood versions where there's a little pumping apparatus in the hand and you're holding on to a knife and as you draw the knife across somebody you squeeze that reservoir and the blood comes out the tip of the knife. That kind of thing is interesting to do."

Another interesting thing about this episode, location manager Russ Hamilton reveals, is where it was filmed. "There was a great western town in Maple Ridge that was built for a TV show many years ago, and we shot out there in the middle of nowhere. It was just a lot of fun." It wasn't always fun getting to the location though. "On a Monday morning — when we were supposed to shoot there on Tuesday — we find the road to get to this location is under four feet of water, and we had to find a way to get the trucks there!"

SAM: So you got sidelined by a thirteen-year-old girl, huh?
DEAN: Oh, shut up.
SAM: I'm just saying, you're getting rusty there, kiddo.
DEAN: Shut up!

The location helped give 'The Benders' a "*Deliverance* subtext," composer Jay Gruska comments. "But I didn't use any banjos... because then it would've been a joke." And this creepy episode was no joke.

"I was surprised at what the network let us do," Shiban admits. "I was sure when they saw the first cut they were gonna go, 'No way, you guys are crazy, this can't go on the air.' But I think it was violent in a good way — violent in a good scary way, in a good horror movie way."

"We really started hitting on all cylinders with 'The Benders'," production designer Jerry Wanek concludes. ✑

Below
Missy calls for
"Daddy".

SHADOW

Written by:
Eric Kripke

Directed by:
Kim Manners

Guest Cast: Nimet Kanji (Pedestrian), Melanie Papalia (Meredith McDonnell), Lorena Gale (Mrs. Dunwiddy)

While investigating mysterious deaths in Chicago, Sam and Dean run into Meg, who is happy to see Sam. He, however, is suspicious of running into her again, so he spies on her and discovers she's behind the murders. Meanwhile, Dean determines the murders were committed by a daeva, a Zoroastrian demon of darkness, which is invisible to the human eye, except for its shadow.

The brothers also learn that the murder victims were from their hometown, Lawrence, Kansas, and figuring they might need help, Dean leaves a message for their father. Sam and Dean go after Meg, but she is one step ahead of them, using her daevas to capture them. She reveals that they're just bait in a trap for their father. Sam distracts her while Dean tries to free himself, but she catches on and stops Dean, which is what the brothers wanted her to do so that Sam could free himself. He destroys the altar controlling the daevas, and the demons throw Meg out of a window to her death far below.

Back at their hotel room, Sam and Dean find their father waiting for them. John hints he's close to finding a way to kill the demon he's been hunting, but then the daevas strike. Meg isn't dead after all, and she has an amulet to control the demons. The family is seconds from death when Sam uses a military grade flare that flashes a light so powerful that it dispels the demons of darkness. They stumble out into the street, where Dean insists that John leave them because he's vulnerable with them around, so they split up once again.

SAM: I think there's something strange going on here, Dean.
DEAN: Yeah, tell me about it. She wasn't even that into me.

DID YOU KNOW?

The warehouse loft used in 'Shadow' was actually a reused set from the TV series *Tru Calling*.

For Jeffrey Dean Morgan, 'Shadow' is an important episode because it sees the Winchester brothers finally reunited with their father. "That whole episode turned out really well. Very fun to do, and emotional and cool, and the episode was scary... so all the stuff we needed to do was there."

For Nicki Aycox, working on 'Shadow' was memorable for a very different reason. "My hardest scene was the scene we shot with the two guys where I had them tied up to the pole. I had to go back and forth and slide across the floor, and get on top of Jared and then turn around and back over to Jensen, and then having my focus back and forth with those guys. And they couldn't move, so I had to do everything. For me, I think that was the most difficult scene to shoot."

Production designer Jerry Wanek also remembers the episode because of the technical difficulties of the shoot. "'Shadow' was an incredible feat just because of how difficult it was to play to something that was totally not there. Every lighting setup, we had to have some sort of surface behind it so that the shadows would play. That was interesting..." Visual effects supervisor Ivan Hayden recalls similar challenges. "It was really trying because we did a lot of blue screen work. We had two great stunt performers provided by Lou [Bollo] on wires in some really good costumes, and some prosthetic makeup gags that we had to tie in together."

"We ended up making quite a few costumes of different 'flowiness' of the arms," costume designer Diane Widas elaborates, "and they did camera tests to see which ones worked."

"[Cinematographer] Serge [Ladouceur] did a great job of coming up with that film noir look; giving us pools of light we could put these creatures into," Hayden adds. "There were times I'm sure that Kim wanted to kill me, where I was on set going, 'No, no, wait, I've got to put up my little tracking marks.' I was running around doing my stuff like a chicken with its head cut off, but I think in the end it was a really good product. And put together with the acting that was involved, it really came out well."

"'Shadow' was one of the hardest things we'd ever done because we wanted to light it in a film noir style with shadows playing a big part in the episode," Kim Manners states. "As the director, I had to design the sequence backwards so that I knew exactly where I needed to have the shadows and what their actions were going to be,

Above
Sam is shocked to run into Meg in a random Chicago bar.

and how they were going to drag Meg and throw her out of the window. And it was very, very difficult for myself, and for Serge, our cinematographer." It isn't obvious to others that Manners was having any difficulties though. "Working with Kim is always amazing," property manager Chris Cooper feels. "He knows what he's doing at all times, which for us is incredible."

SAM: Go to hell!
MEG: Baby, I'm already there.

Stunt coordinator Lou Bollo describes how they achieved one of the episode's key shots: daevas throwing Meg through a window. "In the exterior location where we would have had to have done it, it would've been a really big problem to bring out an airbag and do all that stuff, so they elected to not show the impact and just have the aftermath of it. That was all designed so that in the studio we had the double going out of the window, we had a shot of her breaking glass and falling through frame, and

MUSIC

'Pictures of Me'
by Vue
'You Got Your Hooks
In Me'
by Little Charlie and
The Nightcats
'The New World'
by X

then the idea was that when we look down, we see the body down there."

"That was the first time I got to do Meg," composer Chris Lennertz points out. "I went back and watched what Jay [Gruska] did on 'Scarecrow', trying to make some continuity there. But the thing I think we did with 'Shadow' was we took the scary up a notch because I really wanted her to be noticeably more important and more devilish than all the other monsters." ✍

ERIC KRIPKE'S SHADOWY VISION...

ANGLES ON WALL. Some large, random piles of JUNK cast a large shadow against the back wall. And from this inky splotch —

TWO FIGURES EMERGE. Wraith-like black SHADOWS, in tattered cloaks. TWO DAEVAS.

Like birds of prey, they swarm across the wall. Over both Sam and Dean's SHADOWS (which are projected against the back wall). The boys never have a chance to react —

Sam and Dean each drop to their knees, in feverish pain.

CLOSE ON: Sam's face is scratched, as if by an invisible claw. He SHOUTS out in pain —

Opposite
Dean collects some important information.
Below
Sam notices a troubling connection between recent murders and his hometown.

HELL HOUSE

Written by:
Trey Callaway

Directed by:
Chris Long

Guest Cast: Kyle Labine (Third Teenage Boy), Agam Darshi (Jill), Jay-Nicolas Hackleman (Second Teenage Boy), Krista Bell (Dana), Gerry Mackay (Mr. Goodwin), Nick Harrison (Mordechai Murdock), Jase-Anthony Griffith (Sheriff), Natasha Peck (Second Teenage Girl), Travis Wester (Harry Spangler), Shane Meier (Craig Thursten), A.J. Buckley (Ed Zeddmore), Britt Irvin (First Teenage Girl), Colby Johannson (James)

D ean and Sam are playing childish pranks on each other, but it doesn't distract them from looking into the story of a house in Richardson, Texas, supposedly haunted by Mordechai Murdock, a farmer who killed his daughters when he couldn't feed them during the Depression. Dean is leery of the story's legitimacy, but Sam believes in the sincerity of some teenagers who told a web magazine that they saw a girl's body hanging in the house's basement... even though the body had disappeared by the time the police got there.

The brothers check out the house and discover some freshly painted symbols on the walls. They also cross paths with two wannabe ghost hunters, Harry and Ed, who run the Hellhound's Lair website Sam used to locate the place. When they fail to find anything useful, they leave the house to the "professionals", but that night a teenage girl is hanged by the ghost. The next day Sam and Dean talk to the police, who claim the girl committed suicide. They sneak back into the house and are attacked by the ghost... which they're shocked to discover is immune to rock salt. Dean remembers that he saw one of the symbols on a Blue Oyster Cult album, so they confront the person who first reported the story to Hellhound's Lair, and he admits the story was made up.

The brothers come to the conclusion that one of the other symbols painted in the house, a Tibetan sigil that focuses energy to create a tulpa, caused the legend to take on a life of its own. When they fail to convince Ed and Harry to take their website down, they share a "tip" that Mordechai's spirit can be killed by wrought iron bullets. They make sure the new story is posted for the masses to disseminate, then head back to the house, but the website crashes right after they checked, so the addition to the legend doesn't take and they're unable to kill the tulpa. In a last ditch attempt, Dean burns the house down, and without a real house to haunt, the fake ghost ceases to exist.

Sam and Dean finally call a prank truce — and turn their attentions on Ed and Harry, who head off to Hollywood thinking a producer wants to tell their tale of the "Hell House".

DEAN: I hate rats.
SAM: You'd rather it was a ghost?
DEAN: Yes.

Executive producer Eric Kripke thinks it's a very interesting idea to have an episode about how urban legends are created and spread, and about how they can become

DID YOU KNOW?

Jared Padalecki starred in the movie *Cry Wolf* (2005), which has a plot that involves the deadly contents of mass electronic messages becoming real. While some of the movie's advertisements hint at the possibility of tulpa-type supernatural horror, it is actually more of a psychological thriller.

real. "Not only was it a hilarious episode," Kripke says, "but it's really got some brains to it. It ended up becoming a very meta episode."

The jar that Dean double-dares Sam to eat the contents of is a perfect example of how assumptions and fear of the unknown can make something as innocuous as an old jar of jam seem ominous. "An old mason jar with just a little bit of red liquid in the bottom, aged like it's been sitting there for fifty years, and you don't know what the red liquid is — it could be jam or it could be blood..." teases set decorator George Neuman.

Costume designer Diane Widas recalls fondly the fun her team had creating the look for Ed and Harry, because they were "trying to make them silly. And as much as our boys are serious, trying to make them a little bit more interesting — a little bit geeky without going too far..."

There was nothing silly or geeky about the haunted house's interiors, however, particularly its basement. As Neuman recalls, it's a "creepy old abandoned house in the middle of nowhere. Anything that you can visualize as being creepy, that's what we'd bring to this set."

Despite the creepiness of the house, this episode does focus on laughs. Composer Christopher Lennertz points out that there's a *Supernatural* musical humor motif that has appeared in several episodes, starting with the early bridge scene in 'The

Pilot', that's put to good use in 'Hell House'. "It's the humorous brothers' theme — which is actually this guitar line," he explains. "It's when they're on the case and it's not scary, it's just fun. I wrote it in 'The Pilot' and Jay [Gruska]'s done a couple of versions of the same thing.

"Eric and I have been friends for so long, and we used to make fun of those kids, of the blogger websites," continues Lennertz. "The joke was they'd read something into it that wasn't there. So, when I saw that episode I totally knew what they were going for. One of the things we did with the music was we lightened it up — it was much more of a plucky sound. The other thing that was interesting was that, because the Hellhound's guys were investigating, I got to use more things like triangles and things that were almost like a *Mission: Impossible* kind of percussion in there, which gave a lightness to it. It was a nice change."

The website portrayed in 'Hell House', www.hellhoundslair.com, is a real site that has stories about "The Haunted House", "Road Ghosts", "Creepy Clowns", and many others that'll be familiar to fans of *Supernatural*. "To be honest," Kripke shares, "Hellhound's Lair didn't catch on the way we'd wanted. Anything that we or the network have officially tried to do hasn't caught on nearly as well as what the fans are doing themselves. The way that it's virally spread and organically spread is better than a corporate entity throwing out what the online presence of the show should be. I'd always envisioned an online presence where people discussed and traded urban legends, and talked about the legend from that week's show. It never became what I wanted it to become..."

SAM: That's your solution? Burn the whole damn place to the ground?
DEAN: Well, no one will go in anymore...

As discussed earlier in this companion, Kripke has always enjoyed researching American folklore and urban legends. "It was the kernel of the show that initially fascinated me," Kripke reiterates. "I think it's fascinating from a cultural place, from an academic place. Some of my favorite fan letters are from people who have been turned on to urban legends because of the show. One teacher wrote me that she used *Supernatural* as a way to teach her class on a unit on urban legends and American folklore, which to me was about the highest compliment anyone ever paid me." ⚡

Opposite
The 'ghost' of Mordechai Murdock goes up in flames.
Below
The mobile headquarters of webzine Hellhound's Lair.

A Closer Look At:
REAPERS

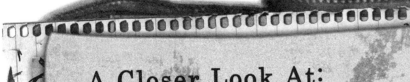

The physical manifestation of death, the personification of this most feared event, is a concept that has existed since the beginning of recorded history. The most common representation of death — aka the Grim Reaper — is a skeletal figure carrying a large scythe, and wearing a flowing, hooded black robe. The origin of this imagery appears to be related to Father Time, since there is a direct correlation between death and aging, and the Greek personification of time, Chronos, is represented as carrying a sickle (due to storytelling confusion with Cronus, a harvest god).

While the thought of death coming for you can be truly terrifying, reapers aren't usually depicted as murderous monsters. They just collect souls. Often they can be quite helpful, aiding the souls on their journey to the next world. Though, while the reapers don't distinguish between good and evil when choosing whose life to take, they still note whether your soul glows black or white, so they know where to take you...

DEAN: There's only one thing that can give and take life like that. We're dealing with a reaper.

SAM: You really think it's *the* Grim Reaper? Like, Angel of Death, collect your soul, the whole deal?

DEAN: No, no, no — not *the* Reaper. *A* reaper. There's reaper lore in pretty much every culture on Earth. They go by a hundred different names. It's possible that there's more than one of 'em.

SAM: But you said you saw a dude in a suit.

DEAN: Oh, what — you think he should have been working the whole black robe thing? You said it yourself that the clock stopped, right? Reapers stop time. And you can only see them when they're coming at you.

"We started with the hood and sickle, obviously," writer Raelle Tucker confirms. "And we were writing these scenes where the guy in the cape walks into the parking lot... and we were like, 'What?' There's just something deeply cheesy about that image. You just can't get past it. And it's not really that scary because we've seen it a million times — people joke about that image constantly. It's not terrifying anymore. So we really were tying to figure out: what would Death look like? We decided he was going to be the most shrivelled old man you could ever imagine. That scared us and gave us chills."

A Closer Look At:

TULPAS

Simply put, a tulpa is a being created by the act of someone imagining it. The most common way this is accomplished is with Tibetan spirit sigils, which are used in mystical customs to focus thought and belief. A monk with intense concentration can create a tulpa on his own, but tulpas can also be created by a group consciousness — such as through people reading about something on a website. Once created, a tulpa has a life of its own, and can only be destroyed by refocusing the thoughts that created it... or by killing its master.

SAM: Kinda makes you wonder... Of all the things we hunted, how many existed just 'cause people believed in 'em?

"The only thing they have in common is their total randomness, because the kids who did it, did it as a prank," says Eric Kripke of the symbols that the Tibetan spirit sigils were buried amongst in 'Hell House'. "They just grabbed whatever symbols they could from different theological textbooks. The whole point was that they didn't make sense when they were all put together. A great touch was that the episode's writer, Trey Callaway, used some symbols from a Blue Oyster Cult album, which weren't even real symbols.

"That episode was based on a true anecdote from Trey Callaway. When he was a kid in Texas, he and his friends went to some abandoned barn and painted the inside with red paint. They put red paint and chains on the table, and started telling their friends that they'd stumbled onto this place where all these murders happened and that it was a true thing. Then kids started going out there to check it out and scare each other. One girl went out and thought she saw some specter attack her, and thought something was chasing after her. She ran away so scared and frantic that she fell and broke her leg. The cops went out there and investigated whether something ever actually happened out there.

"It was the self-fulfilling prophecy of this prank that I found so fascinating," Kripke recalls. "It was really a metaphor for urban legends in the first place. All urban legends are just stories that people tell to scare or warn each other. If they're told enough, if they're whispered through a friend of a friend, these things take on a life of their own and become real."

SOMETHING WICKED

Written by:
Daniel Knauf

Directed by:
Whitney Ransick

Guest Cast: Colby Paul (Michael Sorenson), John Prowse (Manager/"Bud"), Ridge Canipe (Young Dean), Penelope Cardas (Nurse), Chandra Berg (Bethany Tarnower), Erica Carroll (Mother), Stacee Copeland (Nurse Betty Friedman), Alex Ferris (Young Sam), Mary Black (Crone), Adrian Hough (Dr. Aaron Heidecker), Ari Cohen (Miles Tarnower), Venus Terzo (Joanna Sorenson), Jeannie Epper (Shtriga)

Based on coordinates sent by their father, Sam and Dean visit Fitchburg, Wisconsin, where children are falling into comas for no apparent reason. They meet with Dr. Heidecker, who reveals the disease works its way through the siblings in a family. At the house of one of the victims, Dean sees a handprint with elongated fingertips splayed from the palm. He recognizes it and tells Sam their dad has faced the creature before and wants them to finish the job. A witch known as a shtriga is creeping into the bedrooms of children and stealing their life-forces.

The witch is practically invulnerable, but can be killed with consecrated wrought iron when it's feeding. Since the creatures normally take on an innocuous human disguise such as an old woman when they're not feeding, the brothers think they've found her, but their suspect is just a patient in the hospital. When Sam researches past incidents, he discovers that Dr. Heidecker was alive in 1893, but Dean doesn't want to fight the creature in the pediatric ward...

At the hotel where they're staying, the owner's youngest son gets sick and her older son, Michael, blames himself for leaving the window open. Dean wants to use Michael as bait, but Sam won't hear of it until Dean explains that he *has* to kill this monster. When they were little boys, Dean left Sam alone and the same shtriga almost killed Sam... which helps to explain why Dean always follows their dad's orders without question. When the creature comes, they attack, but don't actually hit it while it's feeding, so it leaps on Sam and starts feeding. This time, Dean blows it away for good.

DEAN: Don't worry, I'm sure there's something in Fitchburg worth killing.
SAM: Yeah, what makes you so sure?
DEAN: Because I'm the oldest, which means I'm always right.
SAM: No it doesn't.
DEAN: Yeah, it totally does.

"I have this weird fear of really old decrepit women," executive producer Eric Kripke admits. "Like those old women in wheelchairs with the clouded cataract eyes — that's just a really scary image to me."

Key hairstylist Jeannie Chow enjoyed her role in creating exactly the type of old woman that freaks Kripke out. "We had to make the old crone. That was really fun.

DID YOU KNOW?

Erica Carroll, who played the mother (in the scene in the park) in 'Something Wicked', also played a nurse in the episode 'Faith'. That episode was set in Nebraska, this one in Wisconsin. Perhaps she's a demon following the brothers across the country...

Above

The shtriga sucks out
Sam's life-force

She was sort of our brainchild. Her transformation was a great transformation for Shannon [Coppin] and I. The actress came in as a spry fifty-five-year-old with bright red hair, and they wanted her to look like a derelict, hundred-year-old lady that somebody just sort of left behind in the old folk's home and she hasn't had a bath or a visit or talked to anybody and she's kind of gone senile. That was a great transformation because Shannon and I really got to push the boundaries with her as far as completely changing her look, from being a redhead to having the long gray

Above

Dean receives a troubling phone call.

MUSIC

'Road To Nowhere'
by Ozzy Osbourne
'Rock Bottom'
by UFO

hair, really accentuating her wrinkles, giving her saggy pouches."

Likewise, costume designer Diane Widas had fun creating the look of the witch. "We ended up doing eight or ten of them, and trying to make them look all the same was pretty challenging because it's not like a shirt where it's exactly the same — in order to get the texture and the detail, it's a little more freehand. It was something that we started working on and then we just kept working on it until we ran out of time, and then it was like, 'Well, that's what it's going to be.' I can't wait until I know exactly who we're going to get because if I do then I won't be able to have it broken down as well or I just won't have time to build it. This was a prime example, so we did it thinking that it could be somebody that was seven feet tall or not, so we prebuilt, and then once we knew who it was, we trimmed it shorter. It was really creepy and she was so good, too."

"That was really a fun show to do," recalls composer Jay Gruska. "There was a lot of creepy piano with orchestra music in that. It had a piano motif that repeated throughout." Music editor Dino Moriano comments that the "music and effects

DEAN: Dad never spoke about it again. I didn't ask. But he, uh, he looked at me different, you know? Which was worse. Not that I blame him. He gave me an order and I didn't listen, and I almost got you killed.
SAM: You were just a kid.
DEAN: Don't. *Don't.* Dad knew this was unfinished business for me. He sent me here to finish it.

Above
Dean and Sam use video surveillance to set a trap for the shtriga.

played well together. When the demon leans in, the music builds up to a point, then when it begins to suck, the sound effects take over."

Another element of the story that Kripke really enjoys is the idea of, "What if this was a hunt that the boys were on when they were little and then they had to come back and revisit it? That was a separate element that we'd always wanted to tell a story about, and it just seemed like the perfect opportunity to do that." ✍

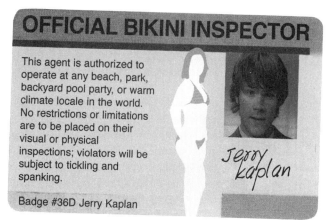

OFFICIAL BIKINI INSPECTOR

This agent is authorized to operate at any beach, park, backyard pool party, or warm climate locale in the world. No restrictions or limitations are to be placed on their visual or physical inspections; violators will be subject to tickling and spanking.

Badge #36D Jerry Kaplan

Jerry Kaplan

PROVENANCE

Written by:
David Ehrman

Directed by:
Philip Sgriccia

Guest Cast: Taylor Cole (Sarah Blake), Keith Martin Gordey (Daniel Blake), Kenton Reid (Waiter), Jody Thompson (Ann Telesca), Jay Brazeau (Darryl), Jodelle Micah Ferland (Melanie Merchant), Linden Banks (Isaiah Merchant), Curtis Caravaggio (Mark Telesca), Barbara Frosch (Evelyn), Josh D. Clark (Workman), Sarah Mutch

A young couple is murdered in their home shortly after buying an antique family portrait painted circa 1910. Sam notices the story in a paper and it matches a pattern his father noted in his journal. The victims' belongings are at an estate sale, so the brothers go to the auction house searching for cursed objects. The owner's daughter, Sarah, flirts with Sam, but then her father kicks the uninvited "art dealers" out.

Dean convinces Sam to take Sarah out to dinner, and she shares the provenances (ownership histories) from the estate sale, which Sam uses to match up the painting with all the murder victims in his father's journal. The brothers break into the auction house and burn the painting, but it rematerializes. They go to see a local historian and learn that the father in the painting killed his family and then himself. Sarah's father resells the painting and Sam, Dean, and Sarah find the new owner already dead. Sam explains to Sarah what's going on, and she reluctantly believes him. They share an intimate moment, but he tells her he can't get close to anyone because he's cursed.

The whole family, except for the father, was cremated, so they burn his body. But when they go to destroy the painting, it's the daughter who materializes and attacks Sam and Sarah, shutting Dean out of the house. Sarah figures the little girl's doll is the key because it has some of the girl's real hair, so Dean goes to the family mausoleum and burns the doll. As the brothers leave, Sarah bids Sam a tender goodbye — and points out that since she's alive, maybe he's not cursed after all.

SAM: So, what are we today, Dean? Are we rock stars? Or army Rangers?
DEAN: We're LA TV scouts looking for people with special skills. I mean, hey, it's not that far off, huh?

DID YOU KNOW?

In a shot of parked cars near the beginning of 'Provenance', one of the license plates is "THE KRIP" which is a reference to *Supernatural* creator Eric Kripke.

For key hairstylist Jeannie Chow, working on the portrait painting was the highlight of the episode. "We did a photo shoot where we dressed the family up in that period, gave them period hairstyles, period clothing and makeup, and then we took a picture of it and turned it into an actual painting. And that one was really fun because I had to make a little doll, a miniature version of the little girl. We had to have specially made wigs for the little dolls. And we had to find these doll parts to actually have her features — her hair color, her skin tone, her eye color. And wardrobe had to make little miniature outfits."

Costume designer Diane Widas also enjoyed designing the little girl's dress and its miniature version. "We originally didn't know if the clothes should be cracked or not because it was an oil painting or if we were going to have to do 'strokes' on the outfits. In the end, we didn't do that."

"I loved the little girl who came out of the painting in 'Provenance' — I think that is super scary," says Eric Kripke. And Phil Sgriccia agrees. "It's really important to get the guest cast right," Sgriccia says of why he thinks it was so scary, "because it does rely on them. [Jodelle Ferland] was wonderful. She knows how to get where she needs to. She didn't have to do a lot other than look menacing, but she was poised."

Sgriccia notes that another perfect piece of casting was Taylor Cole as Sam's love interest because they had such amazing chemistry onscreen, and because she got along so well with Jared Padalecki and Jensen Ackles off screen. "They liked working around each other," he says. "All three of them are from Texas, so that helped. She was kind of a tomboy, so that helped. And she didn't put up with their crap — if they

Above

Sam and Sarah Blake under seige from Melanie Merchant's ghost.

Above

Melanie, looking
deceptively innocent.

MUSIC

'Bad Time'
by Grand Funk Railroad
'Nighttime'
by Steve Carlson Band
& Darren Sher
'Romantic Pieces, No. 1'
by Extreme
'One More Once'
by Black Toast Music

were kidding her, she'd kid right back. So she kinda joined into the club pretty quickly." But Sgriccia couldn't say whether Sam would ever see Sarah again. "I think in our show we tend to try to keep the guys romantic when we can. Sam is more the straight shooter and Dean is more the playboy. It's a little harder for Sam to want to commit to liking somebody in some ways because he's remembering his girlfriend from the beginning of the year. He's a little reluctant to get romantic because he's still holding onto Jessica."

While there had been romance in earlier episodes, composer Christopher Lennertz says, "This one was much more romantic than we'd ever been. I tried not to overdo it, but I tried to make it real. Sam let his guard down, so we let the music play a little more real emotion." Of course, Lennertz didn't focus all his energies on the romance; his score enhanced the scares, too. "Whenever you saw the painting, we would sting it. It was much more classic horror."

For the episode's largest set, "We turned a two-level furniture store, which had a really good look to it, into the back of an auction house... and just filled it with tons of antiques and tons of art," set decorator George Neuman reveals. "You're better off bringing your own antique furniture in from a specific film prop house, rather than going to an actual antique shop. I think it's got a lot to do with the possibility of damaging a super valuable piece of art! And part of it is, say, if they're just doing part of a day in there, then they'll match up the location, like if there's a park nearby for another part of the script."

SARAH: You guys seem to be uncomfortably comfortable with this.
SAM: Well, this isn't exactly the first grave we've dug. Still think I'm a catch?

But it's another set that Neuman remembers most fondly: "One of my favorite things is doing the motels. Each one has a different theme, and trying to pull it off with different colors, wall coverings and different textiles and the bedspread and the curtains and stuff, that's very challenging. I look forward to those. In 'Provenance' we did a disco motel, and it was one of my favorites." ✐

DEAD MAN'S BLOOD

Written by:
Cathryn
Humphris and
John Shiban

Directed by:
Tony Wharmby

Guest Cast: Terence Kelly (Daniel Elkins), Dominic Zamprogna (Bo), Anne Openshaw (Kate), Warren Christie (Luther), Sean Tyson (Trucker), Christine Chatelain (Genny), Damon Runyan (Ted), Brenda Campbell (Beth)

When Daniel Elkins is brutally murdered, it catches Sam and Dean's attention because the man's contact information is listed in their father's journal. They search his cabin in Manning, Colorado, and find a letter addressed to their father. John shows up unexpectedly, and after reading the letter explains that his friend had an important weapon in his possession — a gun with the power to kill all supernatural beings, including the demon that killed their mother. The Colt is not in the cabin, so John deduces Elkins' vampire killers took the gun.

John gets a lead on the vampires and orders his sons to go with him. Sam refuses to be ordered around and he argues with his father until Dean plays peacemaker. They sneak into a vampire lair run by the charismatic Kate and Luther, but before John can grab the Colt, Sam and Dean's attempt to save a captive backfires when she turns into a vampire and screams. They escape empty-handed.

John tells Sam he never wanted this life for his sons, and Sam says they're more alike than John realizes. Using dead man's blood, which is poison to vampires, they set a trap and capture Kate, who John offers to Luther for the Colt. Meanwhile, the brothers clean out the nest. Kate frees herself, and a fight ensues. Just as John is about to lose, Sam and Dean save him, only for Luther to grab Sam as a hostage. But John gets a hold of the Colt and shoots him, ending the battle. John surprises his sons by agreeing they should go after the demon together because they are stronger as a family.

SAM: Hey, there's salt over here. Right inside the door.
DEAN: You mean like "protection-against-demons" salt? Or, uh, "oops, I spilled the popcorn" salt?

Writer Cathryn Humphris "wanted to do vampires from the start. It's such a classic. But Eric didn't want to do it too soon." Executive producer Eric Kripke elaborates. "At the beginning of the year I said we'll never do vampires. I was very reluctant to do vampires because *Buffy* [*the Vampire Slayer*] had that market so cornered. So I really wanted to keep away from it and to really stay with ghosts and demons because that was a way we could create our own identity. Later in the season, once we had our own identity and once we were comfortable that our show was different enough — that people knew what we always knew, that it wasn't a carbon copy — we got a little more relaxed with that. One of the things that fans kept asking was,

Above

Sam and Dean
explain to their father
the importance of
sticking together.

'When are you going to do vampires?' We figured since this was our last monster of the season, let's close on a really classic creature, let's do a vampire!"

Humphris couldn't be more thrilled with that decision. She started off as a writer's assistant to co-executive producer John Shiban, and 'Dead Man's Blood' was her first produced script. "It was incredibly valuable to write with John," she says. Her only small disappointment with the process was that "several stunts were scaled back because we had to keep the budget in mind." She also reveals that the episode "was purely standalone at first. Eric came up with the idea for the gun, but didn't know it was a gun at first. He came up with the idea for a supernatural weapon, and the myth about Samuel Colt seemed like a perfect fit."

"The big prop in season one was the hero gun, the Colt. That was one of the more interesting things I got to do," property master Chris Cooper relates. "Eric had a specific era in mind, and basically we ended up with the very first revolver that Samuel Colt designed — the very first revolver ever to go into production, which is the 1836 Texas Paterson, I think it was called. We have the best armorer in North America here in Vancouver — Falcon Enterprises. They have virtually every gun

that exists, and they're all functioning, and they're all modified to fire blanks safely for the film industry. They went to a gun show in Las Vegas and this Italian manufacturer was there... and they had this 1836 Colt replica in their display!

SAM: Hey, dad, whatever happened to that college fund?
JOHN: Spent it on ammo.

"That first revolver was a powder and cap gun," Cooper continues. "We ended up making a new revolver piece that could take cartridges just for ease of firing for us, and that got incorporated into the story too. There was this montage of the guy making it and there were thirteen silver bullets that go with the gun. We made the silver bullets and engraved numbers into 'em. And we put a pentagram on the handle and a Latin saying on the barrel, and it ended up being a really cool gun. That was definitely the highlight in terms of props for this show."

Composer Jay Gruska particularly enjoyed the scene where the Colt is fired. "That was really fun music to write, because anytime you have visuals go in slow

MUSIC

'Strange Face of Love'
by Tito & Tarantula
'House Is Rockin''
by Stevie Ray Vaughan
'Searching For the
Truth'
by MasterSource
'Trailer Trash'
by MasterSource

motion, the music wants to feel along with that. With rare exception are you gonna do musically hyperactive stuff when there's slow motion visual." Like with the show's visuals, Gruska didn't want his score to evoke memories of *Buffy the Vampire Slayer*. "I didn't necessarily think in terms of what has been a standard in some other great vampire works. It's variations within *Supernatural* as opposed to, 'Let's do this like *Dracula*.'" 🖉

Opposite
Vampire Kate flirts
with Dean.
Below
Dean and Sam stake
out Daniel Elkins'
cabin.

John

If you are reading this, I'm already dead. I don't know who's more stubborn between us, but, well, you know. It's a damn shame to have to say goodbye this way. But if you knew the truth of it, you'd probably have killed me yourself. You see, old friend, I've got the Colt. Least I HAD it — can't right say who or what might have it now. Check my safe, the combination's one you can remember: 3-8-2-11. If it ain't there, just follow the trail of my blood. I really do pray you get the gun. And put a silver bullet right between that bastard's yellow eyes.

Dan

A Closer Look At:

SHTRIGA

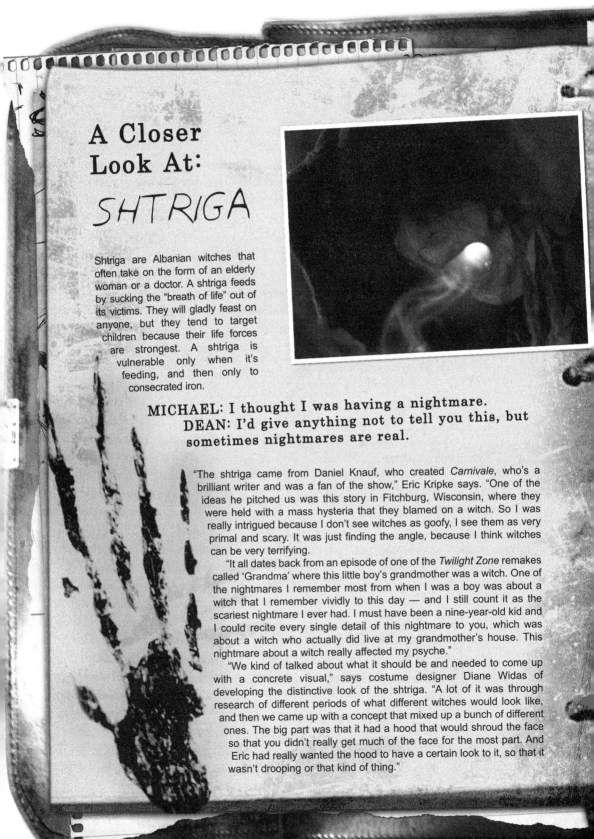

Shtriga are Albanian witches that often take on the form of an elderly woman or a doctor. A shtriga feeds by sucking the "breath of life" out of its victims. They will gladly feast on anyone, but they tend to target children because their life forces are strongest. A shtriga is vulnerable only when it's feeding, and then only to consecrated iron.

MICHAEL: I thought I was having a nightmare.
DEAN: I'd give anything not to tell you this, but sometimes nightmares are real.

"The shtriga came from Daniel Knauf, who created *Carnivale*, who's a brilliant writer and was a fan of the show," Eric Kripke says. "One of the ideas he pitched us was this story in Fitchburg, Wisconsin, where they were held with a mass hysteria that they blamed on a witch. So I was really intrigued because I don't see witches as goofy, I see them as very primal and scary. It was just finding the angle, because I think witches can be very terrifying.

"It all dates back from an episode of one of the *Twilight Zone* remakes called 'Grandma' where this little boy's grandmother was a witch. One of the nightmares I remember most from when I was a boy was about a witch that I remember vividly to this day — and I still count it as the scariest nightmare I ever had. I must have been a nine-year-old kid and I could recite every single detail of this nightmare to you, which was about a witch who actually did live at my grandmother's house. This nightmare about a witch really affected my psyche."

"We kind of talked about what it should be and needed to come up with a concrete visual," says costume designer Diane Widas of developing the distinctive look of the shtriga. "A lot of it was through research of different periods of what different witches would look like, and then we came up with a concept that mixed up a bunch of different ones. The big part was that it had a hood that would shroud the face so that you didn't really get much of the face for the most part. And Eric had really wanted the hood to have a certain look to it, so that it wasn't drooping or that kind of thing."

A Closer Look At:
VAMPIRES

Next to ghosts and demons, vampires are easily the best-known supernatural creatures in existence. Vampires are reanimated humans killed by other vampires who must drink blood to survive. They usually have inhuman strength and speed, and heightened senses, like night vision.

Beyond that, vampire lore is so vast, with so many contradicting variations, that it'd be impossible to say definitively what a vampire is… but the creative team behind *Supernatural* have a clear idea of what *real* vampires are like.

DEAN: Vampires? I thought there was no such thing.
SAM: You never even mentioned them, dad.
JOHN: I thought they were extinct. I thought Elkins and others had wiped them out. I was wrong. Most vampire lore is crap. A cross won't repel them, sunlight won't kill them, and neither will a stake to the heart. But the bloodlust, that part's true. They need fresh human blood to survive. They were once people, so you won't know it's a vampire until it's too late.

"John [Shiban] and I both felt that if we were going to do vampires, we'd have to do our own version, based more on real folklore than what people know to be vampires, which is mostly based on the original film *Dracula* [1931]," says Eric Kripke. "But there's every permutation of vampire throughout every culture since the beginning of time and we got to pick and choose elements that aren't as well known."

"For instance, not every vampire is scared of sunlight, nor does it make them turn to dust," Shiban elaborates. "Certain vampires lived among people, and we figured they could only have done that if they had retractable fangs. We based the fangs on the idea of shark teeth in rows."

"Kate wears a cross around her neck," Kripke points out, "which differentiates us from classic vampire lore. You can't just hold up a cross and expect a vampire to cower away — that's not real. Everything that people know classically about vampires is wrong, so that just gave us an opportunity to plant our own flag and create our own creature."

"We had to make these cocoon-type hammocks out of burlap which were much easier to travel around with than coffins," set decorator George Neuman says of the vampires' new sleeping quarters.

"Dead man's blood was Eric's idea," say writer Cathryn Humphris of perhaps *Supernatural*'s most unusual addition to vampire lore. "I think it's a cool way to subdue vampires."

SALVATION

Written by: Raelle Tucker, Sera Gamble
Directed by: Robert Singer

Guest Cast: David Lovgren (Charlie Holt), Sebastian Spence (Tom), Erin Karpluk (Monica Holt), Josh Blacker (Caleb), Serinda Swan (Nurse), Rondel Reynoldson (Nurse), Richard Sali (Pastor Jim Murphy)

Meg pays Pastor Jim Murphy a visit, and when he refuses to tell her anything about the Winchesters, she slashes his throat. After discovering a pattern of suspicious house fires, John and his sons travel to Salvation, Iowa. Once there, Sam has a waking vision of a woman being attacked by the demon, and tracks her down, but doesn't know how to warn her. Then Meg calls John, demanding the Colt or else she'll kill everyone he's ever cared about... While he listens, she kills his friend Caleb. This is war.

John meets Meg to deliver a fake gun, leaving the real one with the boys to take out the demon. A man named Tom accompanies Meg, and he examines the gun, then shoots Meg with it. John makes a run for it, blocking his path with holy water from a pipe he blessed. Unfortunately, Meg avoids his trap. Meanwhile, Sam and Dean manage to rescue the family from Sam's dream, although the demon gets away.

Tom catches up with John and telekinetically pins him against a brick wall. Dean tries contacting his father, and is worried when he gets no answer. He surprises Sam by telling him that killing the demon is not worth dying over — the three of them need each other. Dean calls his father again... and this time Meg answers and tells him that they'll never see their father again.

> **DEAN: Don't say "just in case something happens" to you. I don't want to hear that friggin' speech, man. Nobody's dying tonight. Not us, not that family, nobody. Except that demon... That evil son of a bitch isn't getting any older than tonight. *You understand me?***

"I wanted to see all the characters mentioned throughout the season, so I decided to just kill off everyone," writer Sera Gamble confides. Her co-writer, Raelle Tucker, expresses the same deadly curiosity. "That's what I wanted to do because secretly I just wanted to meet them. And I knew that the only way that [Eric Kripke] was going to let me meet them all is if I killed them all. The hardest thing about doing an episode about all their friends being hunted down is, what are our guys doing while that's happening? So then we realized that it was going to be an episode that was gonna have two whole separate stories going on at once, and that's a hell of a thing to try to break and write. But when we finally figured out that it was about a child and a replay of 'The Pilot' in a certain way, we knew we'd stumbled onto the right thing. It was like a window that flew wide open to all this emotional stuff with the guys. It just brought back all the themes of the show and tied the season up into a nice big bow."

DID YOU KNOW?

The Latin inscription on the supernatural Colt's barrel, *non timebo mala*, translates to 'I will fear no evil'.

But they still didn't have the story wrapped up. "They hadn't introduced the Colt and nobody on staff knew that it was happening yet," Tucker continues. "We were like, 'Okay, it's going to be our job to be fighting this demon. What are we fighting her with?' And Sera and I were trying to come up with our own versions of what we could do to it. We were getting really frustrated and finally somebody walked in and said, 'We have the perfect weapon.' And the Colt just seems so appropriate for the show. It has an old west kind of feel to it. It's that other layer of, now the story makes sense — we're not just killing your friends because we hate your friends and we want to get back at you (not that that wouldn't be enough reason), we now had something to hold hostage." As much as they loved getting the Colt, with it being central to two other scripts, Gamble points out that it's "challenging to be the middle part of a story arc."

"'Salvation' was different because of the big mythology thing," executive producer

Above

Dean and Sam have a heart-to-heart talk with their father.

Robert Singer comments. "That was more serious, but directing the show is a lot of fun in general. We have a lot of fun on the set. When you're directing, it's up to you to set the tone of what the set's going to be like. I opt to make the best of it: Let's have a good time, get good film, and get the hell out of here as quick as we can."

JOHN: I never used the gun — how could I know it wouldn't work?
MEG: I am so *not* in the mood for this. I've just been shot!
JOHN: Well then, I guess you're lucky the gun wasn't real.
MEG: That's funny, John. We're gonna strip the skin from your bones, but that was funny.

Executive producer Eric Kripke is a big fan of Singer's directing style. "Bob's got an excellent visual eye and he's a hell of a director. And he's the most macho dude ever. Y'know, like I'm a geek reading comic books and he's drinking a Jack Daniels on the rocks on his way to the golf course; he's just a real man surrounded by all these geeks. His episodes have this masculine kind of reserve to them. I'll sometimes overwrite a scene and the characters will get too weepy and sentimental with each other, and he rewrites the dialogue so you're still getting the depth and feeling but it's kind of much more macho and it's not overly sentimental. It's like a good Clint

MUSIC

'Carry On Wayward Son' by Kansas

Eastwood movie, and he brings that to his directing."

Composer Chris Lennertz had fun playing off all the themes from the seasons that were brought back in this episode. "I sort of threw everything but the kitchen sink into that episode. There was a little bit of the elements from all the episodes."

A key theme which was brought back in the episode was, of course, the scheming Meg. "The biggest thing for her was she was traveling and we really wanted her to look like a girl that the boys would be interested in," says costume designer Diane Widas of the evolution of Meg. "They always say, 'Scary Just Got Sexy', about our show, and we do do a little bit of sexy, for sure, but I find with [*Supernatural*'s] producers, they tend to keep the people more real than you do sometimes on young networks where more sex is hanging out. They wanted her to look like she would be appealing, but without necessarily having to be overtly sexual. She's a lovely girl, so we worked off that. As she got stronger, the yellow leather jacket was one that we bought and made to work for her. Then the little red jacket, as she became more demonic, was one that I designed and we built for her, and that was to reflect a little more of her power as she shifted." ✠

Below

Sam and Dean watch their father depart once again.

A Closer Look At:
DEMONS

Demons have been haunting people's nightmares since the beginning of time, or at least since the beginning of practiced religions that distinguish between good and evil. It would take a whole book to describe the numerous types of demons that have been said to exist. In American lore, demons are typically fallen angels that reside in hell, and in order to walk the Earth, they must possess humans. Demon possessions have been blamed for everything from mental illness (such as multiple personality disorder), to murder, to priests having sexual intercourse.

Most demons leave behind a sulfuric residue and are averse to salt and holy water. However, typical deterrents don't seem to bother the more powerful demons — the ones with yellow eyes — but they can be avoided if you pay attention to the warning signs: increased electrical storms and other abnormal weather, temperature fluctuations, and disease outbreaks in animals, which is essentially the Earth itself balking at the demon's unwelcome presence.

But the demons you really have to watch out for are daevas. They're Zoroastrian in origin, and they don't bother with possession — they just go straight for the kill. You can only see a daeva by its shadow... and by then, it's probably too late.

DEAN: Anyway, here's the thing — these, uh, these "daevas", they have to be summoned. Conjured.
SAM: So someone's controlling it.
DEAN: Yeah, that's what I'm saying. And, uh, from what I gather, it's a pretty risky business, too. These suckers tend to bite the hands that feed them... and the arms... and torsos...

"Originally the demons — the classic yellow-eyed demon and Meg and the other demons on our show — were not going to be possessed people," Eric Kripke reveals, "they were going to be their own entities, halfway between spirits and corporeal creatures, that disappear and reappear, that could be these solid things. But then, very early on, once we saw 'Phantom Traveler', we said, 'Well, you know, what works best is if this particular demon can possess people.' And that's the classic conception that everyone knows of demons anyway. So we adjusted to that and I think that was an improvement, because we now have that element of the show where you never quite know who the bad guy is, which I think really helps us. It makes it a more interesting story element as well."

"We struggled a lot with demon rules," John Shiban admits. "Once Meg starts getting active, it starts getting tricky because you have to be very careful that a rule isn't too broad and too easy on you, or a power that's too great for your guys to ever thwart. On the other hand, you have to give them powers that are good obstacles. In the airplane episode ['Phantom Traveler'], they did the exorcism and it didn't work, and I remember we went back and forth on that. Ultimately I think we ended up in the right place, which is: exorcisms are specific. You just gotta be careful when you're making your rules."

SAM: And these, uh, these protective circles, they
really work?
BOBBY: Hell, yeah, you get a demon in one, they're
trapped, powerless. It's like
a satanic roach motel.

"Basically, if there are any two breeds of demons, it's demons and their pit bulls," explains Kripke. "Demons possess people and they're fairly erudite and sophisticated, and I think that draws a nice comparison to our blue-collar heroes. Every so often they have more monstrous, pit bull animal-like demons at their disposal, like daevas, which are Zoroastrian demons of darkness. They're meant to be more savage, primal demons than our demons, which are more snotty and sophisticated.

"The yellow-eyed demon and Meg are so much fun to write. The yellow-eyed demon really made his first appearance in 'Devil's Trap'. He was around, but he was never a character who had dialogue and personality. There's a movie called *Devil's Advocate*, and the sense of humor that Al Pacino brought to his demonic role was great. We really liked the idea that in an episode that's so heavy, let's give the demon a personality and a sense of humor, and a sense of fun — he enjoys what he's doing. Nothing gives me more pleasure than writing one of the demons, because they can be so cruel and so funny; there's nothing they can't say. It allows you to be so mean, but have so much fun with it. Every insult you've always wanted to say, the demon can just say it because that's who he is. Between him and Meg, those two were just really fun characters to write because of how they could talk to the boys and really twist the knife psychologically."

DEVIL'S TRAP: IN DEPTH

Written by:
Eric Kripke

Directed by:
Kim Manners

Guest Cast: Jim Beaver (Bobby), Sebastian Spence (Tom), Matt Riley (Fireman), Guy Bews (Husband), Monique Ganderton (Wife), Chad Bellamy (Mechanic)

Desperate to find their father, Sam and Dean seek help from an old family friend, Bobby, in Sioux Falls, South Dakota. When Meg bursts into Bobby's house, the brothers lure her into a "devil's trap". She claims their father is already dead, and Dean gets violent, but Bobby warns him to go easy because there's an innocent girl trapped inside the body with Meg. Sam starts an exorcism, and frightens Meg into giving up John's location. Bobby points out that since Meg has been shot and fallen from a building, the demon is the only thing keeping the body alive. Dean argues that they'll be putting her out of her misery, and Sam finishes the exorcism. "Meg" is expelled in a rush of black smoke. With her last breaths, the human girl thanks them, and warns them that the demon is using their father as bait.

The brothers go to an apartment in Jefferson City, where they use holy water and salt to subdue their father's demon guards. Tom suddenly attacks and starts beating Sam, but Dean uses the Colt to kill the black-eyed demon. Later at a cabin hideout, a storm whips up and they realize the yellow-eyed demon is coming, so John demands the Colt. But Dean is disturbed by the fact that John is unconcerned that he "wasted" two of the Colt's precious bullets, and he realizes that his father is possessed. The demon mentally flings him and Sam up against the wall, and scolds them for killing his children, Meg and Tom. When Sam demands to know why the demon killed Jess and his mother, the demon responds that they were in the way of his plans to make Sam and the other children like him into killing machines.

The demon tortures Dean, who begs his father for help. John regains control of his body for a brief moment, and this is enough for Sam to wrench himself from the wall and grab the Colt. Sam doesn't hesitate — he shoots his father... in the leg. The demon howls in pain, weakened but not dead. John begs Sam to kill him, but Sam can't, and the demon escapes. But the reprieve is short-lived, for as Sam drives his father and brother to the hospital, a semi truck with a possessed driver broadsides the Impala, demolishing the car and leaving the Winchesters dead or dying...

DID YOU KNOW?

Sebastian Spence, who plays a demon on *Supernatural*, previously played the Devil on the supernatural TV series *The Collector*, in the episode 'The Pharmacist'.

MEG: I swear, after everything I heard about you Winchesters, I've got to tell you, I'm a little under-whelmed. First, Johnny tries to pawn off a fake gun, and then he leaves the real gun with you two chuckleheads. Lackluster, man. I mean, did you *really* think I wouldn't find you?
DEAN: Actually, we were counting on it.

Reflecting on 'Devil's Trap', Kripke muses, "For a season finale, it's not action-packed at all, which I think was an interesting choice for us to make. The episode is two

P.117

Sam uses the Colt to chase the yellow-eyed demon out of his father's body.

Above

The demon is exorcised from Meg Masters' body.

MUSIC

'Bad Moon Rising' by Creedence Clearwater Revival
'Fight the Good Fight' by Triumph
'Turn To Stone' by Joe Walsh

showdowns with two different demons, bookended, and with a little action in the middle. But the dramatic content of the scenes between all of them was so rich, and such monumental things happened, that I think we got away with it."

"I really liked working on the last episode," composer Jay Gruska says. "It wasn't necessarily the most complex or diverse, but it was a good episode. Eric told me to really understate, which I did, like with the low drones that underlined the tension in the scenes."

"The episode, actually, in terms of the writing, came easy," Kripke recalls. "It came easy because so many momentous things were happening. We knew we were going to exorcise the demon inside Meg and that Meg was going to die. And we knew that they had to rescue dad, because that's how the previous episode ended. And we knew that dad was going to be possessed by the yellow-eyed demon.

"At one time or another, each character was the one kidnapped then returned possessed. Production realities end up affecting your creative [decisions], but if you're able to roll with the punches, it makes them better," Kripke continues. "At the time, Jeffrey Dean Morgan was a very difficult actor to schedule because he was on our show and *Grey's Anatomy* at the same time, and shuttling back and forth from Vancouver to LA. He was in first position on *Grey's Anatomy*, so we had to work around their schedule, not vice versa, and they were using him a lot, so it was very difficult to steal Jeffrey away for one or two days to shoot what we needed him to shoot. We quickly realized that it would be impossible to have Dean or Sam kidnapped and have the whole episode be dad and one of the boys rescuing the other son because we knew we simply wouldn't have Jeffrey long enough in our schedule to get all the scenes shot. So fairly late in the process we changed it so it's dad who got kidnapped.

"Looking back, you say, 'Of course, that's how it *had to* be.' The whole year has been looking for dad, so of course the final push of the grand finale of the season would be one last very desperate search for dad. And of course it's dad who had to be possessed by the demon, because all the year the boys have been looking for two people — they've been looking for dad and they've been looking for the demon — and so it makes all the storytelling sense in the world that they'd find both of them at the same time... and that both of them would be in the same body. And the choice that would be presented to them of: 'We can kill the demon, but it means having to kill dad.' The reality of the production motivated us to dig deeper and find the right solution. So much of our job is just these happy accidents — you really have to give yourself over to the fact that things happen for a reason."

Staging the episode's two demon showdowns was a particular challenge. "Shooting that Meg exorcism scene was just really, really difficult," Kripke recalls, "because you have to make it visually exciting when in reality four characters are all just standing talking to each other. And then two days later you're back in the cabin with the demon and the two boys."

Production designer Jerry Wanek remembers thinking the same way. "We were in this one cabin for an extended period of time. That cabin had better be interesting, because we're spending a lot of time in it.

"Because it was all done at night, we had to create an entire forest, and then we had to build the cabin in the forest," Wanek continues, explaining how they created the setting. "So everything that you see in that sequence was all done on stage. We want to keep the audience engaged, so if we do not totally sell to people that this cabin is in the middle of that damn forest, they're going to switch the channel. So for us, that was a huge thing to match the exterior forest. That's the key for that episode."

MEG: He begged for his life with tears in his eyes. He begged to see his sons one last time — that's when I slit his throat.
DEAN: For your sake, I hope you're lying. 'Cause if it's true, I swear to *God* I will march into hell myself... and I will slaughter each and every one of you evil sons of bitches, so help me God.

Jensen Ackles, for one, didn't find it difficult to stay "engaged" while filming the "just standing talking" scenes. "It was cool," he says. "We had Kim [Manners] directing. We really feel safe when he's at the helm. He definitely brings something to the table that ups the level of everything. He gets some good stuff out of us!"

Manners certainly remembers getting a very emotional performance from Ackles. "I'd never shot an exorcism before," he states. "We had a girl tied in a chair. And I wanted to make it exciting, I wanted to give it a lot of movement. We were doing three-sixties and very tight shots. It had to be very powerful. This poor girl — she collapses on the floor and dies in Jensen's arms. It was very, very touching because Dean realized that he killed this young lady who was an innocent victim of this demon. That was an interesting character dynamic."

Nicki Aycox recalls a different element of that arduous shoot. "It was thirteen or

Above

Demon-possessed-
John enjoys
tormenting Dean.

fourteen hours straight, which is actually pretty unheard of in a television show," she says. "Usually, you're going through scene after scene after scene really quick, and that was just one scene, although it was a really long scene. By the end, everyone was very tired and it was back and forth laughing and giddy, and then trying to focus and get back into it. But it definitely got a little bit slap-happy there in the end!"

For Padalecki, Aycox's performance was one of the elements that made the shoot memorable. "Every time I think of Nicki Aycox, I think of the scene after she's been exorcised, and she was sitting there dying. This feels so unprofessional, but I remember during her coverage, when we laid her down on the ground and she was sitting there telling us 'Sunshine Apartments' or something like that, I remember totally breaking character and just looking at her like, 'Man, she's good!' I remember just watching her like, 'Jeez, this girl can act.' So it was real fun to have her around. Plus she's cool, she's another sweet girl." Ackles concurs. "Nicki was great. She definitely brought a lot to the table. I was really sad to see her go at the end of the first season."

As might be expected, the biggest technical challenge of the episode was filming the crash finale. "We did it in an area that used to be an airport space and has flat roads," producer Cyrus Yavneh reveals. "We had to spend a lot of money shoring up the dirt and putting culverts in so that the water would run through it, and then putting the sod on that. It was a one-shot deal, so we did it with multiple cameras. Kim placed the cameras perfectly. To do a shot like that on a television show requires great engineering and thoughtful planning."

In fact, even seemingly minor elements of the climactic scene required thoughtful planning. "We have to get special people in who put in special contact-lenses so that the demon's eyes glow," Yavneh continues. "We're constantly doing tests on different fabrics and materials to see how it glows. And the makeup effects that raised the question, 'Are the boys alive, or are the boys dead?' We kind of learned how to do that as we went along."

"When we broadsided the car, I wanted to have the camera in the car," Manners explains of shooting the crash, "and I wanted the truck to come out of nowhere and hit the side of the car with the camera inside. When we shot the blue screen portion of it with Jeffrey Dean in the foreground, we exploded the window right at him. Well, it's real glass, so to protect that we put a sheet of Lexan in front of it, about a quarter of an inch away from the real glass. Then we put two cannons full of rubber glass below frame. The timing has to be just right so that when we hit the knockers on the real glass and it shatters, we blow the canons full of rubber glass at Jeffrey." (For the detail-oriented reader, rubber glass is "a tin-catalyzed silicone rubber product developed specifically for special effects," special effects supervisor Randy Shymkiw explains.)

"And then, when we cut to outside, we did a very big stunt where the truck was actually cabled on a ninety-degree winch to the car (the car had dummies in it)," Manners continues. "So as the truck was coming at it, it was pulling the car so it had

Below
The power of the
Colt's mystical bullet
courses through
John's body.

to meet in the middle for a center punch. And what I wanted to do was center punch it and hit a canon in the Impala and blow the Impala straight up in the air and at camera and have it rolling in the air." Or, as Kripke describes it, "The Impala was supposed to do a barrel roll — like the worst car accident, like this crazy rolling car accident. The truck was supposed to just drive off into the night, and we see that the truck driver was a demon."

DEAN: Where's our father, Meg?
MEG: You didn't ask very nice...
DEAN: Where's our father, bitch?
MEG: Jeez. You kiss your mother with that mouth? Oh, I forgot, you don't.

But the cliffhanger wound up being just as surprising for the crew as it was for the viewers. "We hit this thing with the truck," says Manners, "the canon went off — it put a hole in the pavement — but the car didn't flip because it was stuck onto the bumper of the truck. Now the truck went out of control and there was a big ravine at this intersection, and just for protection we'd built a plywood and two-by-four bridge. Well, the car got married to the truck, and the truck went out of control. Thank God we had a great stuntman driving it, and he went over this plywood bridge. When I saw them headed in that direction, I thought, 'My God, the truck is going to cave that thing in and it's going to flip the truck, and we're going to have a hell of a wreck.' Well, through the grace of God, that little plywood bridge held, and as luck would have it, the truck started to jackknife and the stuntman saved it. I had a camera in the field in a crash box, so he used his head and he said, 'I'm now gonna push this car right into that camera,' so it went right to black, which was a great cutting point. And that was all the stunt guy who made that decision when he was out of control in this truck, and it worked great."

"It didn't happen at all like we thought it was going to," Kripke reminisces. "But then we looked around at each other and we were like, 'Actually, that looks pretty cool, it looks pretty real.'"

"I was excited when I closed that script up," Ackles recalls. "And I was excited to see the crash, man. I went out there with my video camera on the day and set it up right there with the pylons. And I'm like, 'I'm going to videotape this stuff because it's gonna be awesome!'"

Jared Padalecki was also excited about filming and later viewing the episode. "I was really, really excited and I couldn't wait. I was thinking, 'Man, I hope I can keep my mouth shut and not tell my family,' because I couldn't wait to see their faces or hear their reactions."

Sound editor Mike Lawshe loves the way the sound mix worked out for the big crash scene. "The picture is quadruple cut, and so you see truck, truck, truck, truck. And so you have to make the choice, is it more interesting — and I had to fight for it a little bit — to hear it crash, and then add another crash and add another crash, or the way that my lead editor was doing it on the show and I came up with, which is to intercut it to silence between each crash. So it goes by really fast — there are about eight frames or a little more than a fifth of a second of pause between each of the crashes: 'Cra — Cra — Cra — Cra!' And it makes it worse because it's not just one continual action, it's like it's happening again and again. It's like someone rapid firing a shotgun at your head. It's coming at you over and over again.

"My dialogue editor, Karen, when she first saw it, she just screamed at the screen, and she was like, 'NOOOO!!! I need to know!'"

"We originally were going to kill dad at the end of season one," creator Eric Kripke reveals. "That was planned by about the middle of the year. The reason we made that choice was because looking for dad, in an odd sort of way, is a flaw in the story engine. It was dad off fighting the front line battle and the boys were playing catch up. Dad was actually off having more exciting adventures than the boys, and we believed that

BOOKS, BOOKS, BOOKS.

According to set decorator George Neuman, the set for Bobby's place had around five thousand to six thousand books. "All over the place in stacks, waist-high in books, the entire set. Up the stairs, even. Everywhere you looked, there were stacks of books. Books, books, books."

Below
Bobby's books

Above

John and Sam are
unprepared for the
sudden impact.

was a flaw. Dad needed to die so the boys could move to the front lines, as it were. We needed the boys to be able to explore, investigate and confront the yellow-eyed demon directly. Dad kinda kept the boys one step away from the fight, so we knew we had to remove dad and bring our boys closer to the fight. So originally we were going to kill him — that was going to be the big surprise at the end of the finale. They were going to climb out of that wreck, Sam and Dean were going to be barely alive, and dad was going to die in their arms. But it felt like it would've been the ultimate downer to kill dad on top of everything else, and we just couldn't bear the darkness that it would've framed the show in. So, very late in the draft, we said, 'You know what, we have to cliff-hang it with this car accident. We can't kill him now, it's too cruel to the boys after everything they'd been through.'"

"Being able to film with Jeffery Dean Morgan was awesome," Jared Padalecki says. "Not like it's not fun to work with Jensen, but it's really fun to work with another great actor. He always elicits some response from us that Jensen and I don't get from each other, because when he and I are in character and we're looking at Jeff, he's our dad, and there's just a way you feel when you look at your dad that you don't feel when you're looking at your brother, no matter what. It can only help our character development and the levels of Sam and Dean."

"We've been very lucky with the guest stars we've had on this show," Jensen Ackles concurs. "Jeff's great. Jim Beaver's great." The problem is, as Padalecki points out, they don't stay very long. "It seems like we get a great, talented guest star, and kill them off! It's frustrating, but I guess it goes along with the theme of the show: these two guys making the ultimate sacrifice. We've been pretty lucky, we've had a lot of guest stars who worked very hard."

"I think the season finale was pretty spectacular," co-executive producer John Shiban sums up. "A real nice balance of a cliffhanger and giving the audience a certain amount of answers to what's been going on. I thought that episode was one of the strongest, and I was very pleased because you wanna end on your best footing — especially the first season of a brand new show — and I think we did."

Below

Crew members examine the aftermath of the crash stunt.

SAM WINCHESTER

I gotta find dad. I gotta find Jessica's killer. It's the only thing I can think about.

Jared Padalecki has worked with Warner Bros. since he was seventeen years old. He spent five seasons on *Gilmore Girls*, so he'd built relationships with many executives and casting heads by the time the casting call went out for *Supernatural*... but he almost passed on the opportunity. "Before I read [the script], I was under the impression that since *Angel* and *Buffy* were going out, that they were just going to try to bring up a new kind of campy, fun supernatural-themed show, which, though I enjoy [that kind of show], I didn't necessarily want to be a part of," Padalecki reveals. "But then I had a conversation with McG — because I tested for *Superman* when he was still attached as director, and I knew him a little bit — and he was like, 'No, man, it's not going to be *Charmed*, *Buffy*, *Angel*, it's going to be *The X-files*, it's going to be raw and scary, the real deal where you can develop a character. It's set in reality.'" Fortunately, that convinced Padalecki to go in and audition. "The next thing I knew, they wanted me to meet this guy, Jensen Ackles, and I was like, '*Jensen Ackles*? I have his posters on my wall!'"

Things continued to move quickly from there. By the time he and Ackles tested for the network, there was no doubt he *was* Sam Winchester. "Usually you get in there, and there are four to five guys for your role, four to five gals for the next role..." Padalecki explains, "but he and I were the only two people there. They brought us back in and they were like, 'This is your show.' That's a really nice vote of confidence going in to shoot 'The Pilot'."

From the moment we meet Sam Winchester in 'The Pilot', it's clear he has a strong desire to live a normal life, but once his brother bursts back into his life his very natural hopes and dreams are forced to take a backseat to his supernatural reality. "He's sort of Neo from the *Matrix*, he's kind of like, 'Why me? I just want to have three kids and two dogs, and a two-car garage, and work at a law firm with my wife,'" Padalecki elaborates. "He's sort of the reluctant hero. He's smart, and he's a bit more introverted than I am. He's very premeditative, he's not rash, he doesn't just fly off the handle and do things without thinking it out first."

So Sam's not exactly happy about having to leave his "apple pie life" and run off in the middle of the night to search for his father, who he's not too fond of to begin with... "I sort of resent him," Padalecki comments. "I blame my crazy upbringing — where I'm sleeping with guns under my pillow and seeing things that most people don't even dream of — on him because it's ultimately his quest. And he's driven both Sam and Dean to this life and to do what we do, and so I resent my father for that."

And while he doesn't resent his brother, Sam wasn't exactly itching to join him in

the Impala, either. "There's no hatred there. They're just different. I see myself as different from Dean. 'You want to follow in dad's footsteps, great, that's fine, do it. But I'm not like y'all. I'm not going to follow daddy just because he's daddy and daddy's always right. I don't want to do these things that you want to do. I'm not a both-guns-blazing hero who wants to drive off in a muscle car into the sunset to find the next thing. I want to sleep in a bed in a home, not on a cot in a motel, and live a normal life.' Ultimately, Sam sees his brother and his father as his ties to that life and he wants to do whatever he can to get away from that life."

Padalecki thinks one of the main reasons that Sam doesn't want any part of the supernatural lifestyle is because, unlike his brother, he simply didn't have a relationship with his mother. "He has literally no memory of his mother. He loves her in that she was his mother, his father's wife, and his brother's mother," Padalecki

Adrien van Viersen's conceptual painting of Sam's girlfriend on the ceiling, for 'The Pilot'.

The 'Devil's Trap' truck.

The 'Route 666' ghost truck.

Van Viersen's conceptual painting of the Winchester house on fire, for 'The Pilot'.

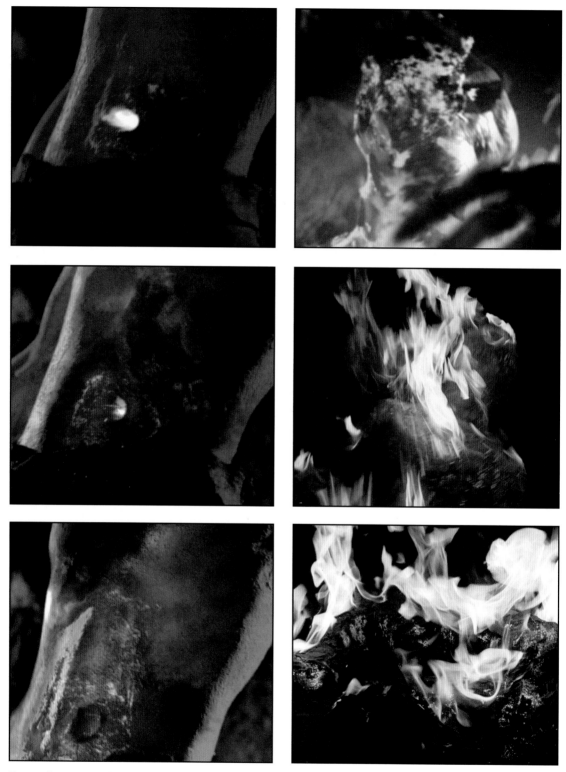

The wendigo goes up in flames.

The homicidal ghost of Melanie Merchant is vanquished in 'Provenance'.

The Mordechai Murdock tulpa vanishes when the Winchesters burn down his 'Hell House'.

Set decorators worked their magic on Riverview to create the haunted Roosevelt Asylum for 'Asylum'.

The church set where Sam figures out how to destroy the 'Hook Man'.

The 'apple' orchard (actually a grove of hazelnut trees) of 'Scarecrow'.

The 'Route 666' motel room.

says. "He understands it, like, 'I get it, mom died, but I didn't know her, I didn't have that same experience.' Dean remembers mom, he remembers her tucking him in and telling him, 'Angels are watching over you.' And he was there that night the house caught on fire and he was carrying me out. I just woke up into this life — as soon as I can remember — where I'm hunting things for reasons I know nothing about."

Only now, those reasons are all too obvious to Sam. He'd been committed to just helping his brother on one last job... until he lost his girlfriend, Jessica, in the exact way his father lost his mother. "It clearly messed him up pretty bad, and obviously it was the turning point that made him say, 'You know what? *Fine*. I'm going to get back in this right now.' But it also cemented Sam's feelings that he's cursed. He has this feeling that people around him, bad things happen to them."

Still, even once he shares his father's burning need for revenge, Sam doesn't charge forward blindly without questioning his fate in life. "I think there will always be a part of Sam that resents what's going on, resents something that he can't even put his finger on," Padalecki muses. "There's always that question of 'How come I got this straw? Why am I able to do these things, get these nightmares and headaches, where I wake up and I see somebody getting killed... and they really get killed? Why me?'"

But he has accepted it, and everything that comes along with it. "He loves his brother very much and, when he mends his relationship with his father, he realizes he loves his father very much. There's a sort of acceptance, which is tough," Padalecki feels. This is Dean's bread and butter, what he's done his whole life, what he excels at, and, in a sense, what he loves to do. Whereas Sam, as Padalecki tells it, would say, "I'm doing this, but I don't love it. I'm not happy with it and I don't want to be doing it. I love my brother and I'm doing it for him, and I'm watching his back and vice versa. I'd rather — if I could go back in time — have nothing to do with this lifestyle at all."

Padalecki sympathizes with Sam's plight, but more than that he respects both Sam and Dean, because they have essentially given up their lives and their happiness to help other people. "It's not like I don't give to charity, or rescue dogs, or wish the best for people... but these guys have made such an enormous sacrifice that there's something to be said for that. 'It's for the better and it needs to get done, so we're going to do it — not just ignore it, not just turn a blind eye, or hope that it gets better, or put somebody else on it. We're going to take care of it.' I really respect that attitude."

Shockingly, at the end of season one, we're left wondering if the Winchesters have made the ultimate sacrifice. "I remember thinking — because obviously you don't know when season one ends whether or not season two is picked up — 'You know what, if we don't come back, at least we died like that, at least that's what took us out,'" Padalecki concludes. "I thought that was a pretty nice way to go. Much better than tripping down a flight of stairs, or something like that!" 🖉

DEAN WINCHESTER

I'll say it again: Demons I get. People are *crazy*.

ensen Ackles was busy working on another WB show, *Smallville*, for which he still had a year on his contract, when *Supernatural*'s pilot director, David Nutter, had him come in and read for the role of Sam. No, that's not a typo, Ackles first auditioned as *Sam*. But after he read for Nutter and Eric Kripke, "They both kind of looked at each other and they were like, 'You mind reading Dean's stuff real quick?'" Ackles recalls. "I took to that more than I did to Sam's part, and right away they said, 'Yeah, that's what we're looking for!' The ball just started rolling really fast, and the next thing I knew they were writing me out of *Smallville*."

When Ackles and Jared Padalecki network tested together, "The whole network stood up and clapped, and said congratulations. It was nice knowing that he and I were everybody's first choice," Ackles reminisces. "Everything felt good. It clicked. We come from very similar backgrounds — both from Texas, similar family lifestyles growing up, both middle children."

Despite Ackles and Padalecki's similarities off camera, in front of the camera their respective characters, Dean and Sam, are miles apart in terms of their outlooks on living a normal life. "Dean is — I wouldn't say the opposite — but definitely the driving force behind getting Sam out of his normalcy and launching him into the world that he's only known because of his father," Ackles elaborates. "He's very driven and he takes a lot after his father's mission — it's pretty much all he knows. He's very blue collar, he's kind of a motor-head, listens to classic rock and drives the old car, and keeps chainsaws and shotguns in his trunk. That's just what he does. That's what he loves. That's his life. He doesn't question it, he just takes it for what it is and loves it because his father loves it. I think that the characters, though they have a different outlook on life and a different mission, they're still brothers and they still share a lot of similarities, and they get to the same decision using a different path."

His mother is the driving force in Dean's life. "Her death sent his father into such a tailspin and he followed down that path. The father figure has really, truly influenced Dean. What he wants and where he's going, and his desires and his needs are all based around the life that his father created for him, that he wholeheartedly accepted. And getting Sam back into that life is something that he wants not only for the manpower on the job, he wants to feel that family connection again, too. I think deep down he wants that sense of normalcy, too, and wants to live a normal life and has the desires that Sam has, just on a different level. He wants more of the camaraderie of that family that he never really got, and that love from a father and

DID YOU KNOW?

Jensen Ackles's father, Alan Ackles, is also an actor. They starred together in the supernatural horror film *Devour*, which was filmed in Vancouver.

brother that he never really got. There's that drive for acceptance that he's truly looking for. He wants his dad to love him, and he wants to protect his brother. It's almost like he wants to do for his little brother what he wanted his father to do for him. He loves him to death, he wants to protect him, he wants to look after him. They're brothers, though; they fight, they bicker, but at the end of the day they've got each other's backs."

Ackles's performance as Dean is so convincing that it would seem the wicked wit and egotism come naturally to him, and he admits, "I enjoy the cocky arrogance that Dean has — it's really fun to play." But the congenial Texan thinks that he would be unwise to act like Dean in real life. "I think I'd probably piss a lot of people off in my life if I was like that. But it's fun to play that 'I don't give a crap' attitude."

To further blur the line, Ackles gives a very Dean-type response when asked what he brings to his character: "Amazing abs." After a chuckle, he adds, "I wish," then he turns thoughtful. "I think that this can be said for a lot of actors — I won't say every actor, but I think a lot of actors — you take a bit of yourself, and expand on it and put it into the character. I know that a lot of characters that I play are a small version of myself, or an exaggerated version of myself in a certain way, an aspect of my personality that I may not totally embody all the time, but is there. Everyone goes through those different feelings. It's hard to say which ones of those filter into the character, but they're definitely there. He's definitely a lot harder and, like I said, a lot more arrogant and cocky than I would be. His love for his family, his convictions about what he does and why he does it, I kind of share those things in my real life too."

That said, Ackles doesn't think he'll ever have a complete grasp of being Dean. "I think that the character, much like us in real life, is ever evolving, ever changing. The different shows add an extra texture, an extra layer to the character. From 'The Pilot' there was something that kind of clicked in me about who this guy was, and then by the third or fourth episode I was starting to feel like I was hitting the stride."

One thing he does grasp about the character is that Dean actually enjoys hunting evil things. "I think he does because it's what he knows he's good at. It's all he's known and it's what he does and where he feels most comfortable. I think that the fact that he's grown up in this [environment] — despite how crazy and uncomfortable it actually is — means this is probably his comfort zone. This is where he feels he is best utilized as a human being for his time on Earth, doing what he was raised to do. He accepts it and takes it on wholeheartedly."

But did Ackles wholeheartedly accept the potential fate that the season finale's script offered him? "I was excited," Ackles enthuses. "I was really excited that it was some big, giant cliffhanger. I thought that was definitely a good way to go. I liked the fact that the three guys were all together, fighting and supporting one another. And even though we're all beat to hell, we're making it together and helping each other and it feels like a force to be reckoned with. So I was excited that they threw us all back together — it was a cool way to end it." ✐

JOHN WINCHESTER

You have no idea how much I want to see 'em... but I can't, not yet. Not until I know the truth.

"Originally I had in my head that I was just going to be doing the one," Jeffrey Dean Morgan recalls of first landing the role of John Winchester. "The idea was to do 'The Pilot'. The kids were a newborn and a three-year-old. I kind of figured that'd be the end of it, they'd have to recast for a father of the twenty-five-year-old... but as it turns out, apparently I play a little older than I'd anticipated on film, so I ended up doing a lot of episodes."

Despite the fact that he's only twelve years older than his oldest son in real life, Morgan still refers to them as "two of the greatest kids I've ever gotten to work with." The sincerity of his words is obvious, as he clearly admires the pair's strength of character. "They're in their early to mid-twenties, and they're so not affected, like a lot of young actors are, by the trappings of what Hollywood has to offer. They remain two boys from Texas that are really just genuinely great guys. I just love 'em. I can't tell you the amount of fun that I had working with them. It was a real privilege. Not an ounce of stupidity in either of them as far as the Hollywood stuff goes."

By all accounts, Morgan himself has never fallen under the sway of "the Hollywood stuff" either, which is probably because he'd never intended to be an actor. He got into acting "accidentally", he reveals. "I was just moving a friend, who was an actor, from Seattle to Los Angeles. I fancied myself a writer and a painter at that point in my life. There was a casting director who thought I should give an audition a try and I did — and I got the role! I happened to love it and realized it was something I wanted to explore." Perhaps there were supernatural forces at work, guiding him into this life. "Do I believe in fate?" he muses. "I believe in fate, but I also believe in a lot of hard work. Yeah, I think there's a certain amount of fate, luck, karma, but without hard work none of it is worth any of it anyway."

While Morgan had little screen time for the first two thirds of season one, he feels that his character was very important to the show. "The boys' quest for the season was to find their father."

Morgan put a lot of thought into how he portrayed the man who had lost his wife in a horrific manner and inadvertently alienated his youngest son. "I played him with extra angst. I think what was on the page, what I foresaw — not knowing where it was going, because no one would ever tell me anything — there was always a lot more going on in his head than he was going to show anybody, including his sons. Because, indeed, there was a lot more going on. He was a tormented soul. Not the best dad in the world; he definitely made a lot of mistakes. I think the key was always that he did things, even when they were wrong, for the good of his sons. He

DID YOU KNOW?

In order to play the guitar for his part in the 2007 film *P.S., I Love You*, Morgan took lessons from Nancy Wilson of the classic rock group *Heart*... which was a dream come true for him since he "had such a crush on her as a kid."

was trying to do right by them, and the process of doing that kind of screwed up his kids a little bit. But amends were somewhat made when all was said and done."

Morgan believes that the key to the first season was the relationship between John and his sons. And he found the cryptic suspense of John avoiding his sons frustrating in terms of developing his character. "It pissed off everybody, it pissed off us as actors, it pissed off the audience watching, because none of us really knew where we were gonna go. But I would tend to at least really make there be more questions than what was on the page, because I felt there had to be a lot more going on in his head than what we even knew, which wasn't a lot."

To give us a further glimpse into what is going on in John Winchester's head, Morgan reveals that what motivates the demon hunter is an "equal combination of revenge and protecting his sons. Without a doubt, it's a quest, a lifelong quest. His wife was killed and that was it. I think his sons — a lot of the time to the detriment of them — became secondary. They maybe weren't first in his line of reasoning or thought, but that changed the more time that he got to spend with them... We don't really know how long they were separated, and that was another thing that was hard to play off. I guess maybe Dean and dad had spent more time together doing some hunting on their own while Sammy was off being educated and stuff. But the relationship we kinda had to forge as we went, not knowing completely what it was. My thought was always that it was about getting revenge for his wife. That was what he woke up and went to bed thinking about. And then I think he came to terms with the fact that he had these sons and he loved them, and then it became as much about protecting them from the threat."

A scene that Morgan finds particularly memorable occurs in 'Shadow'. "The scene

I really liked, that kind of stands out in my head, was when they first meet — where the boys and their father finally are reunited after years," Morgan reveals. "That was my favorite scene that we ever shot, that I ever was a part of in that show."

'Shadow' was directed by executive producer Kim Manners, and Morgan has nothing but praise for him. "Kim's brilliant. He kind of invented the genre with *The X-Files*. There's no better director in doing that stuff than Kim Manners, in my opinion. A lot of the episodes I did were with him, which was fantastic. It doesn't get any better than that — he knows his stuff when it comes to that genre of filmmaking."

Morgan isn't an avid viewer of the horror genre, but he "became more of a fan doing *Supernatural*." Not that this is unfamiliar territory for him. In 2004, he co-starred in the supernatural horror film *Dead & Breakfast*, which featured the tagline, "It's like a bad horror movie, only worse." And he's also appeared in episodes of genre shows *Angel* and *Tru Calling*. "I think growing up we all, or at least I, saw my fair share of monster movies," he sums up.

Morgan looks back fondly on his time on the *Supernatural* set with Padalecki and Ackles: "We were like three idiot brothers. We all turned into six-year-old kids when we were together, which was a lot of fun for us — I don't know how much the crew appreciated it, but we had a wonderful time. I miss that aspect of it."

MARY WINCHESTER

You get out of my house. And let go of my son!

"I just randomly auditioned during pilot season," Samantha Smith states matter-of-factly when remembering how she landed the part of Mary Winchester. "My scene is basically kissing my baby goodnight, and then coming in and seeing this creature over the crib. It was such a funny audition to have to do..." And it's her ability to see the humor in the situation that Smith attributes to her success. "The director, David Nutter, was in the room and I think the reason I got the job is because we were just joking around and we had a lot of fun with it."

Her sense of humor shines through when she describes working with Ackles and Padalecki. "That was really hard, they're so difficult and nasty... No, actually I adore those boys — I would like to put them in my pocket and keep them," Smith confides with a giggle.

She only got to work with Jeffrey Dean Morgan "a tiny little bit, 'cause during most of his stuff, I was dead, but he was lovely."

Despite Smith's brief screen time, Mary comes across as a beautiful person. "I think she was actually very fun and liked, which is where the tragedy of her being killed by such a dark force came from," Smith comments. "She was just all about love and laughing, and loving her children and her family as a whole. I think that, had she lived, we would have seen a much more vivacious person, which is in direct contrast to everything that is going on in the show — she's the beacon."

Smith feels there's more to Mary's death than has been revealed so far on the show. "I think there's the big mystery of why that entity was in the house to begin with, so obviously there was something going on with my husband before my death, because my death wasn't random. I'm not sure, had I not died, whether he would've been a full-time hunter or whether he just would've been avoiding, or what exactly would have happened. So it definitely did change the course of John's life. It seems that Dean is haunted and completely tortured by the fact that his mother was killed. Sam knows that he had no mother [growing up], but he doesn't have the sense of loss that Dean has. And I think the husband never recovered — probably from guilt — not only because he loved me and misses me, but because in some way it has something to do with him and is his fault."

Smith doesn't feel that it is Mary's fault, and is aghast to learn that some fans speculated that her apologizing to Sam in the episode 'Home' was because his birth was the result of an affair she had with the yellow-eyed demon. "No, I can almost unequivocally say that is not the case!" She thinks that the apology "had a lot more to do with the fact that his girlfriend was killed. And because I think it's a foreshadowing of the trials and tribulations that he's going to have because of his

DID YOU KNOW?

To set Samantha Smith's character, Mary, ablaze in 'The Pilot', the crew made a full body replica of her out of wire and covered it in paper maché, and stuck it to the ceiling. That's what they lit on fire. They called her "Christina".

special powers... and as a supernatural entity I'm aware of that and I'm sorry that it's happened to him."

Smith connected to the emotional situation in 'Home'. "I kept feeling like I was going to start crying... and I couldn't, so I had to sort of battle that because it actually touched me a lot, that scene, even though I had like three words or something. The situation of it was very moving to me — to see my sons after twenty-two years, having never met Sam, and then giving my life again for them. I enjoyed that as a moment." ✑

MEG MASTERS

The other day I met this man — a nice guy, you know? We had a really good chat... sort of like this. Then I slit his throat and ripped his heart out through his chest. Does that make me a bad person?

Executive producer Kim Manners handpicked Nicki Aycox for the role of Meg Masters, Aycox reveals: "He called me up and asked if I would want to come do a recurring character that kind of got to throw the boys around a little bit, and I said 'Yeah'." Based on the way the episode 'Scarecrow' concludes, "We knew that it was going to be some sort of an arc. We didn't really have a definitive direction that we were gonna go in, we just kind of knew that we were going to do something that was definitely against the boys — a power that they had to fight. When I got to Vancouver, we sorted that out over time while I was there."

One thing that came through right away was Meg's sexy self-confidence. "I think that when you bring a woman on that's going to be a powerful character, there's definitely going to be some sexuality put into the character. I added a lot of it on my own, but it was definitely in the script as well." Despite a great script, Meg would not have been so memorable without Aycox's impressive acting talents. "Kim and everybody else allowed me to have complete creative run, so pretty much everything you see is what I brought to the character. They just said, 'All right, here are your lines, just go for it, Nicki,' so that's what I did. I wanted to have Meg very stylized and I think that's definitely something I brought to the character."

Aycox thinks that the viewers need to remember that her character was not just an evil monster. "I think it's really important to see that this is just a young girl who was trapped in this demon body, doing all these horrible things, watching it almost like an out-of-body experience. And you see that in the last episode when they finally exorcise the demon from her body and then she's just broken and she dies, and admits all these awful things that she couldn't control. It was very important too, I think, to really show that vulnerable side, because all the way through the arc you don't really see her very vulnerable — she's always sharp-tongued, witty, smart, and always just trying to get what it is she needs and get what she wants. So that, to me, was the most important moment."

She acknowledges, though, that what people seem to like most about Aycox's portrayal of Meg is the delightfully devilish way she delivered her lines. "I didn't really have time to think about it [during shooting], but now that I've seen some of the articles written about the character, Meg, there are so many lines that people found funny. For the 'lackluster' line, right before the exorcism, I didn't really realize

DID YOU KNOW?

Nicki Aycox has appeared on two other horror anthology shows, *The Twilight Zone* and *The X-Files*. She is also known for her memorable turn as Syl on *Dark Angel*, which co-starred Jensen Ackles.

I was putting that much sarcasm in the character. But now that I've stepped away from it, I actually enjoy watching that kind of sarcasm come out of Meg."

Aycox truly enjoyed her time on *Supernatural*, and wants to make one final point. "I think the show is so incredibly special, and I think that comes from who the main actors are. I just wanted to make sure you put in there that Jared and Jensen are absolute dolls to work with." ✍

1967 CHEVROLET IMPALA

DEAN: Unh! The thought of him driving my car...
SAM: Ah, come on.
DEAN: It's killing me!
SAM: Let it go.

"The car *is* its own character," creator Eric Kripke insists. "We always pitched it as the third lead in the show. I understand online they call it the 'Metallicar' and I think that's a funny name for it."

The Chevrolet Impala roared to life in 1958, but in 1967 — the model year featured on *Supernatural* — it was redesigned to strengthen the curves. Right from the teaser for 'The Pilot', which shows John Winchester holding his two sons as he sits on the car while his house goes up in flames, the black Impala has been prominently featured on the series. And shortly after the brothers reunite twenty-two years after the events of the teaser, it's revealed that the trunk holds an impressive weapons cache.

"I didn't know that much about muscle cars when I first began this," Kripke admits. "I originally was going to put them in a '65 mustang. My neighbor at the time pimped muscle cars for a living... and he said, 'That would be the right car if you're a [*bleeping bleep*]. You want a '67 Chevy Impala... because you can fit a body in that trunk.' I got on my computer, looked at a photo of a Chevy Impala and said, 'Oh yeah, *that's* the car.' The goal was a car that when it pulls up next to you at a stoplight, you reach over and lock the door — a car that scares you a little bit, and the Impala is that.

"I love how people have embraced it," Kripke continues. "When I grew up, I loved *Knight Rider* and *Dukes of Hazard*, and the cars in those were as much a part of the shows as the characters. To have a show like that where people connect with the Impala as much as they connect with Sam and Dean, and have it be this iconic image from the show really means a lot to me."

"The first thing we did in 'The Pilot' was say, 'The car needs to have a voice, you need to know it's the car before you even see it,'" sound supervisor Mike Lawshe explains. "We chose things that aren't actually that car in some cases, that are bigger, nastier, have more of a growl to it. Even the tires we do differently than the other cars in the show. We even very specifically chose the door squeaks for the left and right doors."

Dean "loves that thing to death," Jensen Ackles relates. "He inherited it from his dad. That's his life. That's his sanctuary."

Jared Padalecki feels that the car brings back bittersweet memories of Sam's youth. "There was a part in 'The Pilot' where we were just supposed to walk to the

DID YOU KNOW?

The license plate on the Impala is KAZ 2Y5, which is a subtle reference to the Winchesters' home state, Kansas, and the year the show premiered, 2005.

trunk of the car, but I remember finding myself in the moment, looking at the car and feeling, 'Aw, great, on the road again... I remember what this car means — this means I'm going to be sleeping while my older brother's driving and I'm going to wake up in some other place and have some other terrible thing to hunt.'"

"After the season finale of season one, when the Impala got smashed by the semi truck, a few people asked me if Sam and Dean were going to make it, but *everybody* asked me if the Impala would make it," Kripke reveals. "I love that car." ✍

MEET THE CREW

"You're only as good as the people you put together, and we feel we have a very top-of-the-line crew here." — Cyrus Yavneh, producer

Every television show has them. Every television show needs them; no television show would exist without them. They are the crew — the behind-the-scenes heroes. You've heard from many of them throughout this book, but this is an opportunity to take a more in-depth look at what some of them do for *Supernatural*.

Visual effects supervisor **Ivan Hayden** got involved with *Supernatural* right after 'The Pilot'. "A visual effect is anything that has to be done on the computer after the fact," he explains. "At the pre-production stage, I go through the script and I highlight everything that could possibly be a visual effect. Then at the concept meeting stage, we'll go through and say, 'Are you thinking a matte painting here and a wire removal there?' After we whittle down what the main points are going to be, I design and come up with how the execution of the shot should be. Typically it means coming up with the cheapest, fastest, and most efficient way of shooting it. After that we'll do what's called a visual effects/special effects/stunt meeting. The three of us are tied very close together. We'll hammer out what effects I might need the special effects department to come up with. Then I go out on set on the day and make sure that we get all of the information that we need. And I make sure it's executed on the day.

"Also, I'm there to help the director out. They're worried about actor performances, I'm worried about how their performance relates to the effect that I'm going to do. For example, if everyone's supposed to be looking at a spaceship in the sky, I make sure that everyone's looking at the same place. I'm the guy making sure the tennis ball is in the right place for them to look at. Once it's finished filming, and the editors and directors have done their cuts, I'll sit with the editors. 'Do we need to add a little something here?'

"Every show is its own challenge," Hayden continues. "We have to come up with the rules for whatever the ghost or the creature is. We discuss it quite in depth at times. We call it 'Ghost 101'. And if we start getting into more evolved theory, it's 'Advanced Ghost Theory 102'. Ghosts walk through walls — can they open a door if they want to? It's the laws of physics for ghosts! The mandate is that it's 'real world supernatural'. We try to create a rule and follow it.

"'Bloody Mary' was one of my favorite ones — some really creepy scenes. I think that the visual effects really enhanced the show. Those are the ones that I like. You wouldn't necessarily know that it was a visual effect, but it still adds a little bit of that horror beat to what they're trying to do.

"Hopefully it looks real," Hayden concludes. "Visual effects hopes to be the unsung

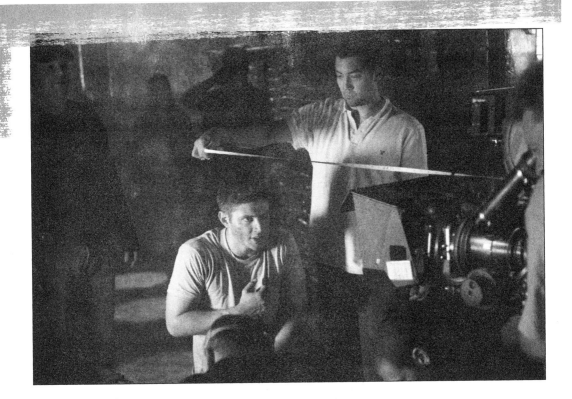

hero, because if nobody notices what we're doing, we've done our job."

"I tend to do these dark, major action shows," costume designer **Diane Widas** explains. "The two challenges of a show like this are: you have to make regular people look interesting, and you have to do a lot of major multiples. These boys live out of the back of their car, so they've got well-used looking items of clothing, so it's not just off the rack a lot of times. You might get your heart set on something specific, but we might need eight or ten of them because they are major action heroes. And Jared is a very tall boy (6'4"), so I end up making a lot of his coats because they're really hard to find in eights and tens.

"For Jensen, he has the journal, so we build a pocket in all of his coats so that he has a place to put that. The boys do have a lot of different clothes. It's like the magic trunk because if they really were what they were they probably would have two shirts and one coat and a pair of jeans, but we obviously have to keep it more interesting for them and for us as an audience. We try not to worry about how many clothes they have in their trunk!

But Widas doesn't just dress the human characters on the show. "We had some amazing ghouls," she remembers of season one. "The wendigo ended up being 7'2" or something like that. We had sort of done leather and Tarzan, and then we realized that it was too elaborate. What we were trying to do was make it so that he fit into the landscape. So we just did a loincloth, and the painting on his body. Running through the woods in bare feet is huge on this show because demons always seem to end up in their bare feet. In this case, we got a pair of neoprene booties and then the

special effects makeup people built feet over them. But I think in the end they didn't really use them... because they looked like booties.

"The Hook Man was interesting because we tried to take an Australian outback coat and make it look not as shiny, but it's not easy to do. We ended up having a paddling pool outside with the coat in the paddling pool in TSP and anything we could find that would remove all the oilskin. For the girls that were working on this, it was really hard to make it look as bad as it did. But in the end it was fantastic.

"It's a great show to design because it's a challenge to make real people look interesting on a regular basis. And we have enough girls that come and go that we get a chance to do a little bit of fashion. We do have a color palette — a little bit darker to help create the mood, unless we're trying to make it happier or a little different."

"I got involved with *Supernatural* quite early because Eric Kripke and I are old college buddies," composer **Christopher Lennertz** reveals. "We went to USC together, and we actually lived in the same fraternity house for about two years. We had the same taste in movies and everything. I used to score all his student films. We did zero budget three-minute short films all the way up to a ten-minute film that cost like $10,000 — and we went to Sundance and won an award with that one, called *Truly Committed.* So when *Supernatural* came up, he sent me a script before it was even shot.

"Then when Bob Singer came in, he had a great relationship with Jay [Gruska], so they said, 'What about switching off with Jay?' We met and got along really well," Lennertz says. "Multiple composers has happened on some really great shows, like *Amazing Stories* and *Twilight Zone.* The nice thing about it is because we don't overlap we both get a little extra time on each show, so I think we get to make it better."

It's arguable that Lennertz's scores don't need to get any better, as his first one for 'The Pilot' received an Emmy nomination. "It felt amazing. It was a big shock to me," Lennertz recalls of his reaction. "I was getting married about a month after the announcement came out, so when I got a call from an old friend of mine who said, 'Congratulations!' I said, 'I'm not married yet,' and they said, 'No, no, no — the Emmy!' The music plays such an integral role in *Supernatural.* To set up something like this musically — something that has a cinematic feel — is important, and I think that's why the show deserves recognition in that category.

"We wanted to benefit from having two composers, but at the same time we didn't want it to feel weird. We didn't want people to say, 'Oh this music doesn't sound like *Supernatural* music.' A lot of people have said that they have to watch the end of the show to see who did which episode because *Supernatural* does have a unique voice."

Lennertz tries to let the visuals inspire the music. "'Dead in the Water' was really well directed and stylized. There were a lot of really cool Hitchcock kind of shots where it'd be a little off-angle and stuff. So for me, I definitely took it as a directive to go a little bit more towards the Bernard Herrmann score range, which is a lot of repetitive dissonant figures and things like that. The other thing that we did in this particular show was go with some vocal stuff where we would pitch down where somebody said 'water', 'die', 'devil' and all this horrible stuff. There was something really gurgly about it, and to me it sounded like water.

"They had these moments in that episode where the kid was drawing and had an emotional connection with Dean. This was the first time that we sort of stumbled upon the real echo-y plaintive piano sound with strings underneath. Eric said, 'That feels like the Winchester emotion.' That became very indicative of Sam or Dean having connections with people.

"Both Jay and I try to find little things like saying the word water and pitching it down an octave, or using a duduk because it sounds like a snake charmer, because to me that's part of the fun of a show like this."

Composer **Jay Gruska** recalls when Bob Singer suggested him to Eric Kripke. "It

Below
Jared Padalecki gets into character.

Above

Padalecki and Nicki Aycox rehearse their lines.

was one of those mildly awkward first moments because Eric has a longstanding relationship with Chris Lennertz, and for all intents and purposes this was Chris's show. Fortunately, it's really worked out great — it's just gone so incredibly smoothly."

When asked what he enjoys most about scoring *Supernatural*, Gruska doesn't hesitate. "An aspect of the show that I've always loved is that even though there are some genuinely scary, frightening moments, there's always a wink in the eye of the writers, the characters, the way it's shot. Eric had such a fun idea, this whole idea of using vintage seventies rock, and he made a point to say that he wants to be very careful that the score rarely if ever crosses into that. But inevitably there are moments where it makes sense to have a crunchy guitar or a big contemporary drum-set rhythm-section sound, even if it's just connective tissue that lasts fifteen or twenty seconds where they don't necessarily want to spend many thousands of dollars to needle drop a song for a ten-second line — which they do sometimes because it's appropriate.

"What both Eric and Bob are great at is the idea that it's always quiet before the big scare," says Gruska. "Even though you don't necessarily follow that one-hundred percent of the time, that's always in the back of everybody's mind. You really try to savor that moment.

"I really enjoyed the first episode I did, 'Wendigo', because there was a lot of music and a lot of different styles. From a strictly musical standpoint, there was big scary stuff and a lot of running through the forest, so that was very percussive and *really* fun to do, with massive amounts of drums and jungle bongs and stuff. And there were also some tender moments. It embodied what I hoped, as my first episode, this show would be, that I'd get to play in a wide musical playground."

However, the series does present some unique musical challenges. "It's not a real theme-based series, even though Chris and I have found ways to reintroduce motifs from previous episodes. It's certainly more work that way because you can't fall back on something you wrote ten episodes ago and go, 'Ah, let me just pop the love theme in here.' Each episode gets treated unto itself. That keeps everybody interested.

"When Chris and I get our first viewing of it, it's usually called a director's cut, which means it's far from locked," says Gruska, explaining the composing process. "It's not locked because the network, the studio, the team here [in Burbank] have yet to make edits and tweaks and it's in a constant state of flux. Most composers are used to writing and having the picture get changed on them once they write a cue, which is always a challenging thing because it's like pulling a thread out of a sweater and the whole sweater could unravel. We usually get to look at the show somewhere within a week of the spotting session, and then we're given about a week, give or take a day or two, to write the score, which ranges anywhere from fifteen to thirty-plus minutes of music. From the second we're done spotting, we're in the dungeon for a week!

"[Supervising sound editor] Mike Lawshe is as good as they come. We always have a discussion about what frequency his sound effects will be in, and that way I'll have a sensitivity to stay out of that frequency range so that things can coexist. There have been many times when there has been full-blown music barreling through something and the right decision is made at the dub to pull the music out and do sound effects. Though certainly what I prefer is when the opposite happens; the truth is that I like it when it just makes for something interesting on the screen. I've been known to sit there at a dub and say, 'You know there was a scene where the music was too loud,' because I'm much more interested in the music being effective than being heard."

For Gruska, it is the entire production team and the atmosphere they create that makes *Supernatural* special. "I've worked on a lot of TV series, and certainly when a show is good, that's a fun thing to do, but when the people that you work with on a show are solid, smart, good attitude, there's sort of a general respect in the air that has to do with 'Everybody's allowed to do their job and there's not a lot of micromanaging.' It's Eric and Bob having this atmosphere of 'We're good at what we do, you're here because we think you're good at what you do, so do what you do.' Here you've got a situation where everybody appreciates everybody else. It's a quality of life thing."

"On top of that you have a show being scored by two different composers and I couldn't think more highly of Chris."

"My involvement is basically being responsible for the look of the show," says **Jerry Wanek**, production designer on *Supernatural*. "Take any given script and, with the collaboration between the director, Eric, and the writers, we'll come up with a plan of what the key story points are and what the tone of the show is, and we'll design from there. What makes this show very different from any other show that I've done is the fact that we have no standing sets. We have a '67 Impala, that's it.

Above

One of the show's more unique motel room designs.

Every episode is a new city, a new state, a new terrain. So there is about fifty percent more building than any other show because we're continually changing locations. For instance, we don't have a police precinct to go to, we don't have a lawyer's office, we don't have a restaurant. We're totally flying by the seat of our pants. It makes the show very unique and challenging.

Wanek has his own opinion on the secret of the show's success. "Because Jared and Jensen have a great chemistry as brothers, what they bring to the table is what makes the show," he says. "After talking to Bob Singer, Eric, and Cyrus, I knew it was going to be a fun show as far as the look. I've done other shows that had great production values but didn't have great casts, and they didn't find an audience and nobody cared about what anything looked like because we didn't believe the characters. I think it's a very tough job for these two young guys to pull this off, but they do it every week, and I'm very proud to be a part of that — it's very special.

"We're very fortunate to have Kim Manners as our producer-director. He's a phenomenal storyteller. It's really important to me to just stay close to Kim and know what his beats are. Because when Kim walks in to tell his story, things better be in the place you said they were going to be and it'd better look the way you said it was going to. He brings everybody's game up to a higher level."

Wanek is particularly proud of the work his team does on the show. "Most shows, you film on stage for maybe two days and you're out [on location] for six. On our show, many times you're shooting five days on the stage and three days out. So that's a lot of sets to build. It's a challenge, but it's great. I am blessed to have the most talented crew in Vancouver, and I spent twenty-some years in LA and I would take this crew over anybody in LA.

"The other thing that has made our stuff look great is the fact that Serge [Ladouceur] is the best director of photography I've worked with," Wanek adds. "He's very fast, which enables us to get a lot of shots. We build it to be lit and we add texture, we add color in certain places for them to pick that up. It's never worked better for me than with Serge and his crew.

"Our job as the art department is truly to create an environment where both the director and the actors can suspend belief — they are truly in that place. We take great pains to go to whatever lengths to make sure every detail is right. When they open a drawer, there's something about that character that's in that drawer, and when they look at a wall, there's a picture there that reflects that character."

Art director **John Marcynuk** has worked with Jerry Wanek for a number of years, on shows like *Dark Angel* and *John Doe*. "I'm involved with the design and execution of all the sets and locations," he explains. "*Supernatural* doesn't have any standing sets, which means we're constantly under the gun to produce a proper dramatic environment for the show. The show is fairly consistent in its look — it's very moody, textural, spooky — but we also like to add as much reality and as much color and interest to our sets as possible.

"We consistently put in sixty-hour work weeks for this show to get things done. There's a lot of scouting involved — we're almost constantly in a van looking for locations. Then come the design elements of whatever locations we chose... if we actually found them. If we don't find them, we end up building them!

When asked about his favorite episode or element of season one, Marcynuk's reply is unexpected. "The motel rooms always provide a lot of interest to us because we're constantly trying to reinvent something that you might find along an American highway. We attempt to make those as realistic and colorful as possible. A motel room is basically four walls and a few beds, but we try to provide an interest in terms of the lighting, the finishes on the wall, wallpaper, and so forth. Oddly enough, a lot of work goes into those.

"I don't have a favorite episode — they're all interesting. It's all part of a big crossword puzzle to get a season done.

"Our element is a very subtle element to the story because we provide these elements that are almost taken for granted, but not in a bad way. Part of that is credence to the quality of work that we try to produce, that one doesn't look at the background or look at something and say, 'What is that?' or 'Where are we?' We always try to make an effective environment, and that helps reinforce the story. In essence, we're part illusionists. What actors do with flesh and blood we tend to do with paint and wood," Marcynuk concludes. "We invent a drama, we invent a character... and I would invite people to enjoy that illusion and reflect on it.

"We create America every week on this show. We're experts, so to speak, at creating the United States in British Columbia."

DO YOU BELIEVE?

Do *you* believe in the supernatural? That is the question I put to the cast and crew of *Supernatural*. My asking the question was probably to be expected, but many of the answers are far from predictable...

"I *want* to believe," Eric Kripke says with a chuckle. "I've never even had anything vaguely paranormal happen to me, and you'd think I was a great big target. And I've stopped having nightmares since working on this show because they're not nightmares anymore, they're just my job. But I love the stories and I *hope* it's real."

"I don't think I believe in it the way we portray it," Bob Singer states, "but I've seen too much evidence to the contrary not to believe that there's something out there. My wife swears that she saw a ghost at our old house! There are phenomena that are unexplainable that I think you have to chalk up to the supernatural. I'm certainly not worried about it, but I believe it."

David Nutter is more philosophical. "In all the goodness and badness in the world... there has to be more behind it than what we see, I think. Our premonitions and intuitions have to have a source somewhere. I think that there's definitely more than meets the eye."

"I believe in some supernatural stuff, yeah," says Sera Gamble. "There's plenty of stuff out there that we can't explain. I'm fairly superstitious as a person, but I've never seen a ghost or anything like that..."

Unlike Gamble, Jensen Ackles is a bit of a skeptic. "I hate to say it, but I think that this show has given me a little bit more courage than I probably should have. A few weeks ago we were shooting at an abandoned insane asylum — where we shot 'Asylum' — and it's an actual place, a place where they did electroshock therapy and all that crazy stuff, and people died (there are scratches on the floors and the doors). I'm just strolling through there with a flashlight like I have no care in the world. I'm like, 'No ghost's gonna hurt me!' I think that there's a part of me that's like, 'Ehh', but there's also a part of me that's not gonna rule it out either."

Jared Padalecki is a believer, but not to the extent that he'll be trying to sneak an EMF meter off the *Supernatural* set anytime soon. "Yeah, sure," he says. "I mean, I don't *not* believe in it. I'm not a believer so much that I'm certain it exists. I'm a believer in the sense that it seems hard to think that it wouldn't exist. There's just a lot of stuff out there that I don't know about and it's a big world and a big universe. Something that could fit under the definition of supernatural is bound to be legit, that's what I feel."

Jeffrey Dean Morgan echoes Padalecki's sentiment. "You know," he says, after a pause, "I think I don't not believe in it. I haven't had any supernatural experiences myself. But, yeah, absolutely, I'd like to believe that."

"I believe in a power greater than myself," Jerry Wanek states without reservation. "I think I'd be an idiot to think this is all there is. I mean, look at what the Hubble telescope sees... I don't believe there are any real coincidences or accidents. The fact that I came from a little town in Wisconsin and got to go to Hollywood and make movies is beyond my wildest dreams when I was that kid in Wisconsin. So anything can happen. I think there's something out there and I just embrace it."

Ivan Hayden looks back on his childhood for the answer. "I certainly remember when I was a kid that things went bump in the night... and you look back at it now and you're like, 'There's still no real logical explanation for that.' I think that when I was raised, my parents weren't telling me ghost stories — I was having nightmares before I was ever told a ghost story."

Kim Manners might suggest to Hayden that it's aliens going bump in the night. "I believe in other life on other planets," he says. "I once saw a ghost. It was just a black thing. It woke me out of a dead sleep when I'd just got out of college. It was at the foot of my bed and it came and hovered over my face, and I got freezing cold... and — I had a roommate at the time, a buddy of mine — I tried to scream and scream and nothing came out. That's the only supernatural thing that's ever happened to me. So do I believe in it? I believe something weird happens out there. It has to."

Diane Widas may have actually had contact with something 'out there'. "I don't know if it's real or a fantasy thing of a child," she says with a twinkle in her eye, "but when I was a little child, between six and ten, I had a recurring dream where I was going to visit a girlfriend of mine that lived [nearby], and I was invited onto a spaceship by little people and they would take me in and I'd be terrified, absolutely terrified. And I had really long hair and they would cut a little hole out of the back of my hair, and sit me in a chair. They were telepathically telling me 'We're not going to hurt you.' They'd drill their little thing, do their little thing, and then they'd escort me off, and I'd always wake up next to my parents' bed..."

"I believe that there are spirits," says Cyrus Yavneh. "There's just too much evidence that people over the years have recorded. I think there's a whole spectrum of life that we haven't uncovered yet, so I think somewhere in there is the supernatural."

"Definitely," Shannon Coppin responds without missing a beat. "I definitely think there's something out there, but I just want it to stay as far away from me as possible!"

"Jeannie more than me has had experiences with spirits that come and visit," Coppin confides. And Jeannie Chow confirms it. "I have supernatural experiences. I see dead people," she says, tongue not quite in cheek. "Yeah, it's definitely out there. For me as a child growing up, the closet was absolutely the 'no travel zone' when I

Above

Roy Le Grange preaches faith, so you needn't fear the Reaper.

was in bed. I could not sleep with the closet door open."

Lou Bollo claims to be very skeptical about the supernatural, yet he's had an undeniably extraordinary experience. He used to baby-sit a little girl for some friends. "Her name was Daisy, and she was about a year and a half old or something. She was the coolest kid; she was funny and had this blonde curly hair and brown eyes and stuff. And I always thought, 'When I get married, I'd like to have a little girl just like Daisy.' So when I got married, and my wife said 'Do you want to have a child?' I said 'Yeah, I want Daisy.' So she says to me, 'That's going to be pretty hard because you can't just dial it in!' And I said, 'No, I think this is what it's going to be.' So... there she was! She was born: blonde curly hair, brown eyes — an exact copy of Daisy. Same eye problem — she had the same lazy eye on the left side that Daisy did. And about eight years later we ran into Daisy's mother and she saw my daughter, and she said, 'Holy cow!' She goes and gets this album and shows us a picture of Daisy at that age. Identical. That to me was supernatural, so be careful what you wish for," Bollo says with a smile. "Nothing bad has happened, though, in terms of how a lot of supernatural stuff here is evil forces..."

Russ Hamilton is not at all skeptical. "There's a reason for everything that happens, and I believe in karma and other forces, I absolutely do," he says. And he shares a story of his recent supernatural encounter while on location. "Hycroft Mansion has been around forever. It's also supposed to be haunted. We were downstairs scouting it and as we were walking out the door, it sounded like the bookcase fell over in the room behind us. It was loud, so it was obvious — it was like ten feet away from us. So me and the liaison went back in the room to see what fell over. Nothing fell over, nothing at all."

Nicki Aycox never really believed in the supernatural before, but she reveals that lately "I've been really watching this psychic detective on Court TV and I'm starting to change my opinion. They get so much information right, so I think there may be something there. I think what it comes down to is always knowing there's probably something bigger than yourself, that there's a greater power, a greater universe. I think it's very ridiculous for us to walk around and think that we're the only thing in the universe."

Samantha Smith definitely doesn't believe in vampires, but she does believe in "some of it. I can't say I was in a haunted house, but I feel like all the times there are noises and every time you get hairs standing up on the back of your neck for no apparent reason, or you feel a cold spot in your house, or anything like that... All those times when any of those little things happen, I feel like there might be something going on that we don't understand."

In the same way Smith eschews vampires, Chris Lennertz doesn't believe in supernatural entities like the Hook Man or Bloody Mary. "I definitely believe more in the ghost vibe. I wish I had this great story about how a ghost came down and told me what to write, but the only ghosts that I've really experienced while writing *Supernatural* are the ones that sit in my computer sometimes and make it crash, which make me very angry, but I don't think they're real."

David Ekstrom, on the other hand, is likely to believe in vampires, seeing as how he's a... (Well, he went off the record with his hairy secret, which I shouldn't reveal unless I want a visit during the next full moon...) But, on the record, he was willing to say, "It's foolish to limit how you perceive the universe, how you perceive the world. I've had some things happen in my life where I've thought, 'That was kind of strange.' You can't really explain that one away..."

People have tried to explain away what's known as night terrors, but when it's regularly happening to you, as it has to Phil Sgriccia, it feels all too real, and definitely supernatural. "I used to wake up in the middle of the night and it felt like somebody's giant hand was on top of my chest, pushing me into the bed. I could only move my neck and my eyes, everything else was kind of frozen. At the time, it really felt like somebody was doing it, and it was a *presence*. I was renting this house, and after I moved out, it never happened to me again..."

Take what you will from these supernatural insights, but if you're being honest with yourself, chances are you'll agree with Peter Johnson, who sums things up nicely. "During the day, when I'm rational, *no*. At night, when I'm alone, *yes*." ✦

SUPERNATURAL REACTION

**"It's unexpectedly smart and unpredictably spooky, and that's a potent combination." —
David Blum, *The New York Sun***

"We're writing a show that we believe is every bit as sophisticated as *Buffy* or *The X-Files*," says *Supernatural* creator Eric Kripke. Hal Boedeker supported Kripke's belief when he wrote in *The Orlando Sentinel* that *Supernatural* is "the scariest series since *The X-Files*." And he added, "*Supernatural* gives two engaging performers the advantage of sharp dialogue, superb special effects and hair-raising plots."

While the fan response has been great, Kripke wishes more people would look past the show's stars' sex appeal. "Too many people are like, 'It's the Hardy Boys with hot guys.' We're so not. It bothers us because we work really hard to make the show good." *Life & Style* commented on this perspective. "At first glance, *Supernatural* may seem like *Buffy the Vampire Slayer* with [very good-looking] boys, but the show has a darker, more grown-up tone and is well on its way to being a standout spooky series in its own right."

"We're in well-trodden feature territory," Kripke points out. When he originally pitched the show, the pitch was, "Hey, you know *The Ring* and *The Grudge* and *Boogeyman*, how they're doing in the box office? Let's do that on TV." That's something that's arguably never been done before. "It is as close as TV has come to importing the kind of horror associated with theatricals, but it combines those spine-tingling moments with camaraderie and mystery," Barry Garron wrote in the *Hollywood Reporter*, vindicating Kripke's instincts.

"The goal every week is it has to be scary," Kripke says, and according to *The Washington Post*, the show has succeeded in that regard. "Some genuine bone-chilling moments will make this series appealing to those who enjoy a good scare." And Bill Goodykoontz emphasized the scare factor in *The Arizona Republic*. "It is flat-out scary. And not just TV-show scary. Afraid-to-watch-the-review-tape-twice scary."

"Of the six new shows featuring paranormal/extraterrestrial themes, the pilot for *Supernatural* is a standout," noted Mike McDaniel in the *Houston Chronicle* regarding the fall 2005 offerings. Len Feldman echoed that sentiment in *The National Enquirer*. "There are a lot of spooky shows premiering this fall... but if you're looking for the coolest and scariest of the bunch, the natural choice is *Supernatural*." It's saying something that only one of those other new shows lasted an entire season. "Some of those shows were a little too similar to the *Lost* formula," comments Kripke. The difference, he feels, with *Supernatural* was that he didn't approach it as a market opportunity. "I've always wanted to do this show — I like to think some of that passion and enthusiasm made it to the screen." *Newsweek* agreed when they wrote, "Every network wants to get 'Lost' now, but most of the knockoffs are too busy trying to spook us to tell a good story. Not this one." Hal Boedeker summed it up best in *The Orlando Sentinel* when he said, "*Supernatural* is the most entertaining hour from any broadcast network this fall."

While the favorable press reaction has been gratifying, the average viewers' opinions are even more important to Kripke. "I'm fairly obsessive about checking out the message boards after an episode has aired," he admits. "Fan boards really are valuable as real-time audience testing. If you find that every person on every message board everywhere hates one particular element, it makes you pay attention. Or, if you find out that everyone everywhere loves a particular element, then you know you have something good."

Above
Dean pays attention to what the media has to say.

A crisp widescreen DVD box set of the first season came out in September 2006 to a strong response. "They did a terrific job," Kripke notes. "I insisted on a couple of Easter eggs because I look for that stuff myself." There's a commentary on 'The Pilot' by Kripke, with director David Nutter and executive producer Peter Johnson, and a commentary on 'Phantom Traveler' by Jared Padalecki and Jensen Ackles. Along with unaired scenes, a gag reel, exclusive website content (featuring the original pilot script), and a still gallery, there's also two never-before-seen shorts, 'Supernatural: Tales From the Edge of the Darkness' and 'Day in the Life of Jared and Jensen'.

Unlike most young shows, the merchandise for *Supernatural* didn't begin and end with the DVD set. Inkworks was quick to bring out a line of trading cards, which features cards that have a piece of a costume (previously worn by the show's stars) embedded into the card. "The response to *Supernatural:* Season One trading cards has been great!" enthuses Allan Caplan, president of Inkworks. "There is clearly a passionate and interested fan base out there for *Supernatural.*"

Executive producer Bob Singer knows firsthand how passionate the fans are. "Our office in Vancouver is just plastered with postcards. People that are into the show are really into it." ✍

22 Reasons Not To Go On a Road Trip With My Brother

by *Sam Winchester*

1. His car only plays cassettes. Seriously.
2. He picks the worst spots to camp — you're likely to get eaten alive, and I ain't talking mosquitoes... (Fortunately, Dean will go first, because apparently he tastes good.)
3. You'll lose your love of swimming.
4. He stops at the worst places to shop for clothes.
5. He tends to antagonize the police.
6. You never know whether you're giving the keys to him or an evil shapeshifter.
7. He wouldn't know a good cup of coffee if it bit him on the ass.
8. He'd rather squat in an empty house than go to a motel, and then he hogs the bathroom.
9. Road trips are great, but he never wants to go home.

10. You go the slightest bit stir-crazy and he no longer trusts you with a loaded gun.

11. You have one little disagreement and he doesn't hesitate to leave you at the side of the road.

12. Even if he dies, he'll still be a backseat driver.

13. He has a bad habit of playing chicken with ghost trucks.

14. Objects in the rearview mirror may be *less natural* than they appear.

15. He's no help in a fight — he can't even handle a thirteen-year-old girl.

16. His downstairs brain is always impairing his upstairs brain.

17. He's very careless with where he leaves his itching powder.

18. When you think he's watching your back, he's off playing video games.

19. He forgets his wallet in the most inconvenient places.

20. He accepts roadside assistance from vampires.

21. He lets minor roadblocks — like fire — keep you from reaching your destination.

22. "Road kill" takes on a whole new meaning.